Many Pebbles to Make a Difference

Inspiring Ways You Can Improve Children's Lives

by Making Connections

Dear Dana,

For Families, Parents, Grandparents

Please continue to share your Pebbles. I love my Hair.
Warmly,
Julienne

By Julienne Levy Marks

Dedication Page

My book is dedicated to the children and adults, especially the parents I have known and worked with through the years and all the people that I have learned from on our journey through life. Thank you for your continual love and support!

TABLE OF CONTENTS

Chapter 1

INTRODUCTION

QUOTATIONS

"We write in response to what we read and learn; and in the end we write out of our deepest selves." Andrea Barrett.

"How do we teach a child, our own or those in a classroom, to have compassion; to allow people to be different; to understand that like is not equal; to experiment; to laugh; to love; to accept the fact that the most important questions a human being can ask do not have or need answers." Madeleine L' Engle, *Circle of Quiet.*

"Memory is a child walking along the seashore. You never can tell what small pebble it will pick up and store away among its treasured things." Pierce Harris.

WHY IS THERE A NEED FOR THIS TYPE OF BOOK: RE-SOURCE BOOK, HANDBOOK, REFERENCE BOOK, INSTRUCTIONAL BOOK, GUIDEBOOK?

This Book is about *connecting* parents and grandparents with their children of different ages through philosophies and *programs,* activities, experiences of all kinds. As a former Youth Services librarian, museum educator, teacher, and parenting workshop leader, I would often be asked by parents or caregivers for suggestions to help their children in such areas as raising self-esteem, reading, behavior, schoolwork, relationships with others, sharing empathy and compassion for others, being kind to others, etc. I also was asked to help them with their Parenting skills. Many of the *programs* suggested in this Book evolved because of these questions. These *programs* worked for me. They may not work for you. But perhaps they will trigger ideas for you.

I have seen many changes and yes, many things have stayed the same during my lifetime. I believe children are children and the developmental steps have not changed. This Book will share some of my ideas, experiences, concerns and support for families, parents, grandparents. It will also give concrete ideas for successful educational, cultural, and literary *programs* that I have been using in different environments (milieus) designed to help us *connect* with our children. These *programs* deal in some way with kindness, empathy, compassion (walking in someone else's shoes), *connecting*, humanity, sharing our world with each other, the desire to help others, interdependence, *communicating* and inspiring others to see their differences, uniqueness, specialness, but also their similarities.

In our fast-paced technological world, I strongly feel we need to stop and listen to the birds and smell the flowers again. I also believe we need to read, listen to music, go to museums to see artwork and our history, attend plays, play, plant gardens, cook, have fun, and share this with our children and grandchildren. Some of my *programs,* activities, experiences deal with these items also.

I feel/see/hear that the participants in my *programs* are appreciative of me sharing the workshops and my experiences with them. I am receiving the "inner" reward of seeing the children and adults excited to see me, enjoying the books and workshops I share with them, and sharing who I am. I believe this "inner" reward is what we need to "share/give" to our youth.

I have the very strong need in my life to share my experiences, *programs,* philosophy, ideas; therefore, I am writing this Book.

Pebbles

Narrator Neha Gupta explains that "one person, no matter how small, can effect widespread change in the same way as a small pebble in a pond. My experience has made me appreciate the power of the ripple effect.

We've all experienced the ripple effect. You throw a *pebble* into a pond and then watch as that single small action creates wider and wider waves throughout the water. I am throwing out *pebbles* to families, parents, grandparents, making circles larger and larger. That one small *pebble* becomes the source of a much broader outcome."

I see a few ways of thinking about *pebbles* in the context of this Book. In this Book, I will be sharing some of my personal *"pebbles"* (personal philosophy, passion, ideas, strengths, gifts, specialties, activities, *programs*, etc.) that are important to me. Some you may agree with, others you may never have thought about, and others you will reject. If some do resonate with you, feel free to use.

Each of us can share "our" personal *pebbles* that will make ripples and then a difference in our world and others. I believe one's life and what one does, can change a child's life. Send out many *pebbles* making a difference and *connections.* Isn't that why we are here on the Earth — to help others?

Children also need a foundation which can begin with small *pebbles*.

Children may have a special *pebble* and feel that it gives them strength or courage by touching it.

This Book is sharing who I am and my work successes with families, parents, grandparents.

My hope for you, that after reading/perusing this Book, you, the reader will be able to share your ideas/gifts, your specific *pebbles* that are meaningful to you, to "your" parents, grandparents, and their children. There will never be another person exactly like you. These *programs* need your special touch. Take the ideas and *programs* in this Book and put your unique touch/spin on them by being authentically you. Take your ideas and fly with them. I hope my *programs* are an impetus for you to share your gifts. I want to support and encourage you to *connect* in humane ways by sharing your personalized *programs* and ideas to make a difference in your community. I want this Resource Book, Handbook, Reference Book, Instructional Book, Guidebook to support and encourage you in your uniqueness. This Book is interspersed with my personal work life to make it more real and doable. This Book is meant to be used over and over again.

Let these *programs* trigger you or give you a shot in the arm to share aspects that speak to you and/or give it your personal stamp to make up your own *programs*. Use these *programs* as beginnings, additions, subtractions, making up your own or use the *programs* that impress or touch you and make them yours to resonate you and your specific populations, ages, amount of time for a *program,* etc. and then it will become yours. My goal for you the reader is to reveal your own heart by thinking outside the box and challenging the norm by re-thinking assumptions. In this Book, I am sharing from my heart practical skills/techniques/methods to "go" to your heart. To me, being human means having or showing interest in or concern for the welfare of others. Awareness (concern) is the first step to changing. I want this Book to share with you a positive attitude in looking and acting towards others, by being the best of yourself. I want this Book to help you, the reader, be a guide, mentor, and motivator who sparks and offers your child an invitation to have fun and learn, which strengthens, enhances and/or rekindles a child's natural interest and curiosity in learning about herself/himself and the world. I will be sharing some suggestions to help make your life with your children more meaningful and more supportive of who they are through these *programs*.

Connections

"*Connecting* with others is the single most important thing we can do for our happiness."
Connect is defined as interdepend, interwoven.
"The human *connection* is so important. Our children not only depend on us for safety and love, but they depend on us physiologically (the body functioning well.) As parents we need to give dozens of points of contact each day. From kisses, hugs, verbal affirmations, eye contact, and our full attention. Children not only desire, but need these *connections*." I have found that many adults and children are looking for ways to *connect* and re*connect* on our journey of life. *Programs* can help. Many of the *programs* you will be reading about in this Resource Book, Handbook, Reference Book, Instructional

Book, Guidebook concern *connections.* I strongly believe human eye-to-eye contact (face-to-face) that can be found during such *programs* is valuable both for parents and their children. Sadly, many of our *connections* today have us tapping at keyboards, tablets, and phones through screens and machines. As parents, *connection* and contact with our children is paramount.

Communication

The definitions of *Communication*: "*connection* between people or places" and "exchange of thoughts."

To me *communication* is both the talking to others and them listening to you.

It seems some of our *communication* is not humane both to ourselves and to others. In this Book I will be sharing *programs* and ideas that may help with humane *communication*, positive self-esteem, and helping others.

Please see **Chapter 2** under *Parenting Communication Workshops, How To Talk So Kids Will Listen™* and *Siblings Without Rivalry™* both by Adele Faber and Elaine Mazlish and Technology Talk under Parent Seminars in **Chapter 4** for more information on utilizing *communication* in workshops and talks.

Sadly, many of us are not joyful. Henry David Thoreau said, "Most men lead lives of quiet desperation and go to the grave with the song still in them."

Please also see a beautiful and meaningful song about this topic, *Let your Music Soar* by Ed & Gaia Tossing *Heartsong.*

As parents and grandparents we can help our children "Be Themselves."

Maslow's Hierarchy of Needs

In my personal, as well as my professional life, my experiences as a librarian, teacher, museum educator, human being, wife, mother, grandparent, sibling, daughter, friend, member of various groups, etc., it seems that most people regardless of their age want to feel: loved, approved of, respected, important, belong to someone or something, etc.

Maslow's Hierarchy of Needs is a theory in psychology that Abraham Maslow proposed in his 1943 paper "A Theory of Human Motivation," which he subsequently extended. His theory contends that as humans meet 'basic needs,' they seek to satisfy successively 'higher needs' that occupy a set hierarchy.

Things kids need most

All kids need the basics of life - like food, warmth, shelter and clothing. But they also need to feel loved and secure. By giving our children all the things they need, we can help them be safe, be strong and to thrive.

THE SETUP OF THIS BOOK

I believe this Resource Book, Handbook, Reference Book, Instructional, Guidebook can be read through or used periodically when needed, offering practical advice and guidance as it contains resource ideas, philosophy, *programs*, relevant books and materials for families, parents, grandparents. Please note that books are continually being published and the lists of books offered here are not exclusive. There may be many more books on specific topics available.

One suggestion for how to use this book is to skim through it, find a topic, idea, philosophy, *program*, quotation, etc. that you are interested in, then read it, and perhaps try doing the *program* and see if it works for you, adding your own ideas. If not, let it go and try some other *programs*. Trust yourself. Some things may work for you, while others will not.

Not only will I be sharing *programs*, ideas, and books, etc., I will be sharing relevant Stories that may be helpful for parents, grandparents, and/or children, (I would have found it quite helpful to have a story at my fingertips, one I needed to tell, write or share something on a theme.) books, poems, articles for more substantive information on something I have written about, quotations, and websites. By listing websites and articles in this book, I am sharing something about them that I want to share. But they may contain parts I do not agree with. It is up to you to decide what works for you and what doesn't. Please also note that websites do change.

Sharing books and articles with you to back up what I am writing about helps give you validity in making changes if it is needed for your policy, *programs*, philosophy. Sharing is one of my strengths. Find out what your gifts are.

The books shared are for different ages and maturity levels. I have included both fiction and nonfiction books. I personally believe the art work is very important and I only wanted to share books with beautiful illustrations. Sometimes I choose not to use a book if the artwork was cartoon-like. At times, however, the storyline was so excellent, I did share the books even with cartoon-like pictures. I also like sharing books with photographs. In many cases a photograph can show us realism. Your and my opinion about a book may vary which is fine. You decide for you what works or resonates! That is why it is so important to read the book to yourself first before sharing it with your children as you know them. Sometimes, I would find that there were a few "gems" within a book or some books had great sections. Therefore, I often would not share an entire book, just the parts I felt worked. I also found that many books, even if published a while ago, were still so "Right On!" There are also many adult books listed in this book.

I have tried to make this book as user-friendly as I can. He/she and Youth Services Librarian and Children's Librarian are used interchangeably in this book.

I have shared many quotations, so that you have many to choose from and that can be used at different times. Therefore, the book could be used again and again throughout being a parent and grandparent.

The anecdotal, oral, and written parts of participants' letters which I have called **Feedback** about the *programs* and about me shared in this book validate and show you that when you are authentically you, you may get positive results; plus the important need for these types of *programs*. I will also be sharing *programs'* **Agendas** and **PR (Public Relations)** to give you more ideas. I have been quite lucky as I had co-workers who were very proficient with computers and put together informative and colorful **PR (Public Relations).** Thanks to: Gail, Robyn, Carol, Julia, Shannon, and Deborah, women I worked with who helped and taught me more than they realized. Throughout the book, I have written Thanks, and the name of the person who helped/shared this with me in parenthesis.

Sometimes, one needs to quickly find a fresh, new *program* adding your ideas. For example, I would have greatly appreciated easy accessing of wording for many of my *programs*. Hopefully you can find some *programs* here that will trigger you to make up your own.

In writing this Book, using the computer was wonderful and extremely helpful. By using the Internet, I could find the correct spelling of words, articles that would validate what

I would be sharing with you, book titles, and websites where one can find more information about a topic.

The facts that I have shared with you are the way I remember them.

This book includes lists of books. Sometimes I would just use the last name of the author. You can check the Internet or a library catalog to see what the book is about and/or bibliographical information.

Many of these books can be found in your local public library. Some may be in your child's Media Center, online, or in thrift stores.

Originally I wanted to have this Book published by a publishing company. But after many rejections, I decided to self-publish. I wanted to share a part of what a publisher said which gave me hope.

"There is much to admire in your manuscript, particularly its mission. And you sound very eager to get your message out."

My husband and brother had both encouraged me to write separate Books on the different topics for the different populations. I felt one Book would be the most beneficial for the reader. Then my publisher suggested the same thing as my husband and I finally agreed that was the right way to go. So now instead of a 600 page Book there are four Books with the title *Many Pebbbles to Make a Difference: Inspiring Ways You Can Improve Children's Lives by Making Connections.*

For Families, Parents, Grandparents

Education in Different Environments, For Teachers, Librarians, Museum Educators, Parents, and All Who Work With Children.

Reading And Books, For Parents, Teachers, Librarians, and All Who Work With Children

Multiculturalism And Peace, For Teachers, Librarians, Peace Educators, Parents, and All Who Work With Children

My hope is that you, the reader, will put YOUR mark on the ideas in this Book and make them yours.
I am very sad that I need to state the following below: Disclaimer: I offer this information as a guide only. I cannot be held responsible for the actions of others as a result of this information. I am not to be held responsible for the misuse of any information in this Book.

I found the following books and/or websites useful to me:

http://boysread.club/534/no-app-can-replace-your-lap/ Mark, 9/30/15
www.youtube.com/watch?v=T6kndgqeSuk (Heartsong)
http://www.cyf.govt.nz/info-for-parents/the-ten-things-kids-need-most.html
http://www.a-better-child.org/page/888950
https://www.goodreads.com/author/quotes/53005.Andrea_Barrett
http://www.upworthy.com/heard-of-the-ripple-effect-these-young-people-are-proof-that-good-can-just-keep-growing
Thoreau: www.goodreads.com/quotes/8202
izquotes.com
http://www.pbs.org/thisemotionallife/topic/connecting
www.amazon.com
https://en.wikipedia.org/wiki/Maslow's_hierarchy_of_needs

Chapter 2

ABOUT THE AUTHOR, MRS. MARKS

QUOTATIONS

"I am only one; but still I am one. I cannot do everything, but still I can do something. I will not refuse to do the something I can do." Helen Keller

"I am only one, but I am one. I cannot do everything, but I can do something. And I will not let what I cannot do interfere with what I can do." Edward Everett Hale

It is so interesting how the two quotations above are similar but quoted by two different authors. Many of us have similar ideas to others.

"This is my simple religion. No need for temples; No need for complicated philosophy. Your own mind, your own mind is the Temple. Your philosophy is kindness." The Dalai Lama

"Three things in human life are important: the first is to be kind; the second is to be kind; and the third is to be kind." Henry James

"If you can't say something nice, don't say nothing at all." Bambi (But I believe it is important to recognize/express ones' negative feelings without hurting yourself or others and not to keep them bottled up.) (Thanks, Devyani)

"You see things; and you say 'Why?' But I dream things that never were; and I say 'Why not?'" George Bernard Shaw, *Back to Methuselah*

"Life isn't about finding yourself. Life is about creating yourself." George Bernard Shaw
(One of my daughter's favorites. Thanks, Elissa)

"The time is always right to do what is right." Dr. Martin Luther King Jr., *Letter From Birmingham Jail*, 4/16/63

"If you see someone without a smile, give them yours." Dolly Parton

"Light the Corner where you sit." A patron gave me this as a magnet.

MY CAREERS

I have been so lucky to have had a myriad of educational experiences throughout my work career. My educational background helped me to be in the following positions: a youth services librarian (primarily in public libraries but also as a media specialist), teacher (in an elementary school, college, and teaching conflict resolution), museum educator, Motivational Teacher, *Parenting Communication Workshops, How To Talk So Kids will Listen™* and *Siblings Without Rivalry™* both by Adele Faber and Elaine Mazlish, chairperson (the materials I used are in this **Chapter**), youth advisor, and camp counselor. In my career life, I have worked in several educational environments: schools, a college, museums, libraries, camps, and youth groups; have been a consultant to various people and groups; and worked with all age children and adults. I have also developed and codeveloped various *programs* for children, parents, teachers, and camp counselors. I enjoy mentoring others and often we become friends.

When I was teaching elementary school, I felt out of touch with teenagers. I therefore decided to become a volunteer youth advisor for teen girls at two different times and groups. My husband and I attended several conventions. These experiences helped me when I became a mother of a teen.

Feedback

"Julienne Marks served as a "volunteer" professional staff member with our agency for many years, also attending several conventions. She served as an advisor for two groups. Julienne was respected and loved by all her girls. She was always an asset to our Convention staff." (Thanks, Arlene) (Regional Director of B'nai Birth Youth Organization)

My education includes a Master of Arts in Library and Information Science with an emphasis on Youth Services, a Master of Arts in Education, and a Bachelor of Arts in Elementary Education and Sociology. I am continually reading Children's and Young Adult books, books and professional periodicals on Children's Literature, books and articles on education and parenting, as well as having taken relevant classes in my professions.

MY PERSONAL PHILOSOPHY

I believe children are like flowers ready to bloom in their own way. The care of a person and a flower are similar. Give them foundation, sun, water and food. Nurture, listen, talk, and love them at times, and leave them alone to grow at their own rate and way.

People's uniqueness can be encouraged as they learn about themselves and the world around them. Their appetite for life, learning, and knowledge must always be nurtured. I also believe that learning is a wonderful lifelong experience that helps to make life fulfilling and can bring much joy, happiness, and fun to one's life.

Each child is precious and unique and that idea needs to be danced and celebrated. Yet, human beings also have many commonalities. We are all important and we are *interconnected* with all living things. Encourage the child's individual imagination and creativity by supporting the child's potential, guiding it to be released. Have him/her experience the joy, happiness, wonder, and fun that are in the world. Encouragement of a child's interests by sharing with her all forms of information: written, oral, experiential is one way for her to grow. The above builds a child's positive self-concept, an important key in the learning process. Although this was taken from a brochure I produced when I was a Motivational Teacher, it also applies to parenting and grandparenting.

SOME THINGS I QUESTION OR THAT CONCERN ME

I have many concerns that I will be sharing with you. What are some of your concerns?

o   I don't think it is a good idea to ask children to ask for money for their sports team, schools, religious schools, or scouts (Yes, those Girl Scout cookies are really delicious.) and then the children get gifts. *Children and Fundraising: Saying "No" to Fund-Raisers* by Elizabeth Tranel Halverson, *Newsweek*, May 20 1996.

o Treatment of animals is important to me. I, from an early age, chose not to attend circuses or zoos, feeling why should we train animals to do things that entertain human beings?

- Using animals in circuses: *Elephant Cries Tears of Joy as it Walks Free after Fifty Years.*
- I told my parents I didn't want to go any more to circuses since the animal parts were too painful for me. (performing unnatural activities for animals to make us laugh???) Later on, my husband took my daughter alone. She thought about it and decided also not to go. She wrote a report for school about finding information on how horrible animals were being mistreated in many circuses, etc. She also wrote a letter to a local circus about letting the animals go free because of their treatment.
- Zoos are also a problem for me. Yes, I know it is helping endangered animals and today there are not the small cages but zoos still bother me.
- *The One and Only Ivan* by Katherine Applegate and *Saving Lilly* by Peg Kehret are two relevant children's books on this topic.
- Testing animals for medical cures, makeup, etc. also bothers me terribly.

o I don't understand sports whose goal is to hurt people (for example boxing, football and participants screaming, "Get him down!") or using animals in a hurtful way. (like for example bullfighting or cockfighting)

o Why in professional sports do we have the participants compete with each other? Why not let people just share what they can do? (For example in ice skating.)

o Why is there "killing someone" in our games like hangman? I do not understand the popularity of hangman whose premise is to hang a person, and children play it.

Many people unfortunately have experienced others being hanged. I feel the game is not respectful of human life.

o Someone at work, knowing me, sent me a website which is no longer available, of a young man's alternative to hangman (Thanks, Julia).

o Instead of playing hangman Mr. Cebulski came up with an alternative about cave exploring is another example.

o Other examples include the board game, "Clue," and some of the plays that children attend like Theater Murder Mysteries. Murder is used in such an "easy" way. Why?

o Why do we "Sell" to children via TV, etc. that death, hurting others, and kidnapping is not important and is okay? For example, there are postcards and letters children can write like blackmail letters. It is called "Blackmail Postcards by Perpetual Kids." Does that make sense???

o Sometimes I believe that our culture is brainwashing our parents in the schools, many extra curriculum activities are encouraged, many tests, pushing, how important money is, etc.

o Why are Reality TV shows, sports figures, and celebrities' lives so popular? What about our own life?

o Is criticism, even constructive, necessary/useful/ helpful to anyone?

THINGS ABOUT ME/MY TRUTHS

o I am in process of my life's journey and sharing my story. I have many questions.

o I have a deep love for children of all ages. Working with children fills my heart.

o Becoming a parent deepened my understanding of children. Becoming a grandparent to a boy deepened my understanding of boys.

o I am very sensitive and I feel things deeply.

- Many parents have been appreciative of my sensitivity as a teacher and librarian as it may help their children see that although it is not easy being sensitive, one can really feel and then do for others, which can really help our world.
  - I might cry at a book I am reading.
  - I might be quite sad about a news event.
  - I might be quite upset if children are hurting each other.
- I often see both (pros and cons) sides to an incident. I am also a Libra, seeing the scale on both sides.
- I did not like supervising. I don't like to judge others; I didn't want to be on a jury for that reason.
- Being supervised by wonderful supervisors (Thanks, Andy and Jo) helped me to become a better supervisor (in camps, libraries, and museums in training others). What I learned from my supervisors:
  - Being encouraging of whom you are supervising to be authentically themselves even if that is a risk.
  - Utilizing staff's strengths and gifts
  - Keeping my door always open
  - Listening and supporting
  - Showing appreciation for what the staff does orally and by writing notes and utilizing administration thank yous if available
  - Having meetings often with staff. Elicit ideas from staff giving them the credit.
  - Helping the staff, if needed
  - Delegating
  - I personally would rather work in a team with no supervisor.
- I seem to make *connections* with people and will travel to see and go to them. For example, doctors, dance teachers, hairdressers, car repair places, etc.
- I meet people (at a park, office, classes, etc.) and we become friends. I find this so interesting.

o Most of my life, I have enjoyed writing notes or emailing people about things happening in their lives, both positive and negative. Many people say it is so kind of me and they so appreciate it.

- "I just received your note which brightened up my day. Thank you for your encouragement. How sweet you are. These notes are so appreciated and so uplifting." (Thanks, Cindi)
- "Thank you for your note. It was a thoughtful gesture. You are so organized to remember me." (Thanks, Susan)
- "All the great thank you notes you always give everyone, even for the smallest things. You are showing your appreciation." (Thanks, Sandra)
- I asked the elementary teacher at the *Waldorf School* I was volunteering at when I retired, if it would be okay, to occasionally write each student a short letter noting something they had told me which had happened to them. For example, I might write about a new sibling, a new pet, a broken wrist, a visit from Grandmother, a kindness I had observed them doing with another student, commenting on a story they had written, etc. Many of the children really seemed to love receiving these hand-written letters. Some of the children would write back to me. I kept a list of whom I wrote to so everyone in the class received a letter. Please see My Book, *Education in Different Environments,* under *Waldorf Schools* and camp.
- "Mrs. Marks, I liked getting your note about my broken arm." (a child who attends a *Waldorf School*)

o Since I am an older sister to fraternal female sisters, I am quite clued into twins and their siblings. I would approach twins and a sibling and their parents when I worked in the library with concern for the other child getting enough attention.

19

o I like helping children to see their inner beauty and uniqueness
o I so enjoy talking deeply or about "real" things about our world, individuals, our spiritualness, etc. I find it so enlightening and invigorating.
o I like to encourage myself and others to accept others' diversity through multicultural children's literature, music, and pictures. I believe meeting others in the celebration of differences and commonalities is quite important.
o Integrity and the truth are quite important to me.
o I was a vegetarian for several years for ethical reasons. I joined PETA, People for the Ethical Treatment of Animals. There is also a component for children.
o Wherever I worked/volunteered, I would ask for a letter of reference/recommendation for my personal files. This plus other materials from where you worked/volunteered could be put into notebooks so you have a lasting memory of your work places. One can also do this for special occasions like special birthdays or parties. One can look through them at "low" times rereading them to feel good about one's accomplishments or for sharing with future employers.

- One can also keep a portfolio of one's work including **Agendas**, presentations, yearbooks, copies of letters of commendation, awards, newspaper articles, etc.
- Using page protectors, one can keep important papers for presenting to other organizations to **PR (Public Relations)** your *programs*. It could include letters of recommendations, **PR (Public Relations), Agendas**, photographs, the curriculum, etc. I have done this several times.
- I found that sometimes people said very commendable things about a *program*, etc. and I might ask them if they would like to put it in writing.

- Because of this and saving many things, this Book has concrete examples I could share with you the Reader. This Book is also what I am remembering about my work life and my perception of what was true for me.
- Through the years, I have been called a nonconformist. I danced to a different drummer. I trusted my heart. Often I was the only one doing some things. For example, as a teacher I was the only one with an open classroom in my school and as a librarian I offered *Parenting Communication Workshops, How To Talk So Kids will Listen™* and *Siblings Without Rivalry™* both by Adele Faber and Elaine Mazlish. In my personal life, I left my hair grey and didn't whiten my teeth. I felt proud of my years and my body. "If a man does not keep pace with his companions, perhaps it is because he hears a different drummer. Let him step to the music which he hears, however measured or far away," by Henry David Thoreau.
- I took many of the personal pictures and artifacts I had placed in my classroom and libraries and now I have them back in my home. In fact many visitors to my home state, "Your home is like a museum plus you have wall to wall pictures. Every space is taken up with these things on your wall."
- While growing up I was: a twirler in elementary, junior high, and college, a Girl Scout, and a member of a Youth Group.
- I was asked by a friend if her daughter could interview me regarding her college assignment which was titled "Administrative Ethics." The interview helped me to validate my thoughts and my ethics. For example, I said, "I don't like the word Mistakes. I would rather use the word Opportunities. I made a lot of mistakes and apologize and try not to do the same thing again. When others make mistakes, I try to be understanding

about things in the person's life that may be going on and are distracting." (Thanks, Abby and Rose)

- Since this Book is about my work life, it was interesting that I was asked by somebody in graduate school to do a "Career Development Analysis." I answered questions about my dominant values in my home of origin, schools attended with the major subjects taken, and extracurricular activities. Also included was information about my jobs, present interests and hobbies. It made me really think about my work life and its influences. (Thanks, Jennifer and Tom)
- I am honored when people talk to me about their problems and joys. I feel I am a good listener.
- I believe: like many philosophers and songs. "Love is the answer." Check out the lyrics to *"Love Is The Answer"* by Todd Rundgren.

o Someone wrote about me, "Remember you are a kind, gentle being who is dedicated to the benefit of others. The light of this dedication and caring can't help but shine through." (Thanks, Ellen)

o I think it is important to be accepting and nonjudgmental of myself and others. I work on this everyday. Having mutual respect for others for all cultures, religions, races, physically and/or emotionally challenging, ages, gender, etc. to me is a goal I strive for.

o When one feels good about oneself (high self esteem), one doesn't need to be a bully, or jealous of others, or hurt another, or prove oneself at the expense of others.

o I believe that one needs to get stroked (complimented) by oneself and doesn't need it from others. (even though it is so nice to get stroked by others.)

o It is okay to disagree.

WHAT I AM DOING IN RETIREMENT
(for parents and grandparents)

When I retired from being a Youth Services Librarian I wanted to give back to the community. I made a list of what I loved and what came out was that I wanted to continue working with children and parents. And that is exactly what I have been doing.

I have been the chairperson at many venues such as a *Waldorf School*, Hindu Temple, YMCA, private organizations, homes, and libraries while working and in retirement for the *Parenting Communication Workshops, How To Talk So Kids Will Listen*™ and *Siblings Without Rivalry*™ both by Adele Faber and Elaine Mazlish.

The PARENTING COMMUNICATION WORKSHOPS
I Have Used

For many years, I have been using several commercially bought workshops to complement my work. I hope these will be helpful to you on your journey, as you make up your meaningful programs. Be Yourself!!!

Two workshops I have used are the *Parenting Communication Workshops, How To Talk So Kids Will Listen*™ and *Siblings Without Rivalry*™ both by Adele Faber and Elaine Mazlish. Giving this workshop is one of my favorite *programs* to share with others. I myself have learned so much from the parents. We teach what we need to learn.

When my daughter was two in 1980, (my grandson was born in 2006) my husband and I began attending a monthly Parenting group led by Zelda Gross (Thanks, Mina) who had studied with the late child psychologist Dr. H. Ginott. His philosophy was a very humane, acknowledging one. "His greatest contribution and continuing legacy may be teaching the *communication* skills that help parents relate to their children in a caring and understanding way without diminishing parental authority." Some helpful information to check out more about Dr. H. Ginott's work is under *Lessons.*

Later I found the books, *Liberated Parents, Liberated Children: Your Guide To a Happier Family, How To Talk So Kids Will Listen and Listen So Kids Will Talk* and *Siblings Without Rivalry* by Adele Faber and Elaine Mazlish. Faber and Mazlish also studied with Dr. Ginott. They were so impressed with his philosophy that not only did they write the above books; they put together workshops kits of several weeks, including workbooks, to share with parents with a chairperson who facilitated the workshop. I have been that chairperson for many years in Florida and in Georgia. I am passionate about sharing this workshop and have been doing so for many years. Because I used this humane philosophy with my daughter and grandson, as well as in my daily communication with patrons and staff, I saw that it works and I really believe in it.

For many of the evening *programs,* my husband would co-chair with me. Having a man was quite helpful both for the women and men who attended. He explained many of the skills, techniques, guidelines, philosophy quite well. He talked about having a tool chest on your shoulder filled with different ideas that one could use with different children at different times if they resonated with you. What was interesting is that when I began doing the *workshops* with the young Moms I mentored who wanted to become chairpeople, one of them always spoke as my husband sharing the above. (Thanks, Anne)

How To Talk So Kids Will Listen Workshop™
by Adele Faber and Elaine Mazlish

This seven-session 90-minutes *Parenting Communication Workshop, How To Talk So Kids Will Listen™* is based on the book of the same name. "The goal of the workshop is for parents to communicate more effectively with their children" by learning skills in a fun and inspired way through the use of audios, role playing, and exercises.

"How To Talk Parenting" Workshop

PR (Public Relations)

A Sample Flyer

How To Talk So Kids Will Listen™ by Adele Faber and Elaine Mazlish *Parenting Communication Workshop.*

Learn how to communicate more effectively with your children. This hands-on workshop is designed to benefit parents of children of all ages. It is based on the book *How To Talk So Kids Will Listen & Listen So Kids Will Talk* by Adele Faber and Elaine Mazlish.

Julienne Marks

_____, will be the chairperson of this workshop. Please contact _____for more information.

These 90-minute sessions will be offered on the following dates _____.

Session 1: Date: Helping Children Deal with their Feelings
Session 2: Date: Engaging Cooperation
Session 3: Date: Alternatives to Punishment
Session 4: Date: Encouraging Autonomy
Session 5: Date: Praise and Self Esteem
Session 6: Date: Freeing Children from Playing Roles
Session 7: Date: Final Review

Preregistration is required. This workshop is for adults only. Please find alternative arrangements for your children, we cannot be held responsible for your children.

Participants are encouraged to supplement the workshop content and activities by reading the following books: *Between Parent and Child* by Dr. Haim Ginott, *How To Talk So Kids Will Listen & Listen So Kids Will Talk,* and *Liberated Parents, Liberated Child: Your Guide to a Happier Family* both by Adele Faber and Elaine Mazlish.

Following is more of an explanation of each session of *How To Talk So Kids Will Listen*™ from Adele Faber and Elaine Mazlish's website: www.fabermazlish.com.

- **"Helping Children Deal with Their Feelings:** An exploration of what happens to children when their feelings are denied. Specific skills that help children to recognize and cope with their negative feelings: disappointment, envy, frustration, resentment, anger, etc. Ways to accept children's feelings, limit unacceptable behavior, and still maintain goodwill."
- **"Engaging Cooperation:** How children react to commonly used methods to get them to cooperate: threats, warnings, orders, name-calling, sarcasm, lecturing, etc.

Five ways to invite cooperation that will leave parents and children feeling good about themselves and each other."

- **"Alternatives to Punishment:** How do children normally react to punishment? Is it necessary to rely on punishment as a means of discipline? Some alternatives to punishment that enable parents to express their strong disapproval, as well as encourage children to assume responsibility for their behavior."

- **"Encouraging Autonomy:** Ways to help children become separate, responsible people who can one day function on their own. Specific skills that help children to become more self-reliant."

- **"Praise:** An exploration of the kinds of praise that build a positive and realistic self-image, and the kinds that are counterproductive. A variety of ways to help our children become aware of their strengths so that they can put them into action."

- **"Freeing Children from Playing Roles:** A look at how children are sometimes cast into roles (bully, whiner, dawdler, mischief-maker, etc.) and how we can free them from playing out these roles. Six skills that help children see themselves in a different and more positive light."

- **"Final Review (Audio Workshop only):** 'Back-to-life' workshop session; a chance to consolidate what's been learned by applying all the skills of the previous sessions to current problems with children."

During the last session, called "Final Review," we take the philosophy and techniques and try and solve participants' concerns together as a group. We also review the **Reminder Cards** (see below for an explanation) and discuss which ones specifically helped the parents. The last thing I do at this last session is read from *How To Talk So Kids Will Listen & Listen So Kids Will Talk,* page 239 What's It All About Anyway?

Siblings Without Rivalry™ Workshop
by Adele Faber and Elaine Mazlish

This six-session 90-minute *Parenting Communication Workshop, Siblings Without Rivalry™* is based on the book of the same name. "At last it's no longer necessary for parents to grapple by themselves with the problems of sibling rivalry. Now for the first time they can get together, share their frustrations, and study the basic principles for reducing conflict and generating goodwill among brothers and sisters."

PR (Public Relations)
A Sample of Flyer
Siblings Without Rivalry™
by Adele Faber and Elaine Mazlish
Parenting Communication Workshop

What increases hostility between children? What attitudes decrease the hostility? ... will be the chairperson of a six-week 90-minute workshop based on the book *Siblings Without Rivalry* by Adele Faber and Elaine Mazlish that will help you help your children learn how to live together.

During each session, parents will learn and practice specific skills to reduce conflict between their children."

The 90-minute sessions will be offered on the following dates:

Session 1: Date: Helping Siblings Deal with their Feelings about Each Other
Session 2: Date: Keeping Children Separate and Unequal
Session 3: Date: Siblings in Roles
Session 4: Date: When Kids Fight
Session 5: Date: Problem Solving
Session 6: Date: Final Review

Preregistration is required. This workshop is for adults only. Please find alternative arrangements for your children, we cannot be held responsible for them. Call today to register!

Participants are encouraged to supplement the workshop content and activities by reading *Siblings Without Rivalry* by Adele Faber and Elaine Mazlish and *Between Parent and Child* by Dr. H. Ginott.

Following is more of an explanation of each session of *Siblings Without Rivalry*™ from Adele Faber and Elaine Mazlish's website listed at the end of the **Chapter.**

- **"Helping Siblings Deal with Their Feelings About Each Other:** What happens to brothers and sisters when their hostile feelings about each other are ignored or denied? Four specific methods for helping children express their negative feelings to each other without doing damage."

- **"Keeping Children Separate and Unequal:** How siblings react when they are compared to each other - unfavorably or even favorably. Effective alternatives to comparisons. How siblings feel about always being treated equally. Ways to treat children unequally and still be fair."

- **"Siblings in Roles:** Why brothers and sisters are often cast, and cast each other, into different roles. A look at how powerfully these roles affect their relationships with each other. Skills that free each child to become his or her most whole self."

- **"When the Kids Fight:** What can you do when fighting breaks out between the children? An exploration of commonly used strategies that backfire. A chance to practice the skills that reduce rage and motivate children to work out their own solutions."

- **"Problem Solving:** A method for helping children deal with the problems they can't work out for themselves. A simple ten-step approach that enables adults to sit down with the young combatants so that they can move toward resolving their conflicts."

- **"A Final Review:** Time to review and consolidate your skills. Exercises give you practice in applying everything you learned to potentially explosive situations. Finally, an opportunity to take a second look at your own adult sibling relationships from your new perspective."

Part of these sessions is taking a look at the parents' siblings' relationships. Many of the patrons felt this was a most welcome addition to the classes. I did also.

For the longest time I didn't chair *Siblings Without Rivalry™* because I had an only child and I didn't feel I could do the workshop justice. But parents persuaded me to offer it due to my parenting experiences, as well as being one of four siblings. I am very glad that I did as I learned so much, and it really seemed to help the participants.

For Both *Parenting Communication Workshops*

To the workshops, I would add music to set the mood in the beginning of each session, offer relevant children's books, cartoons, and share experiences from home and work.

This is a participatory workshop. I have had participants tell me they do not want to role play, read, etc. That is fine with me.

Several of the sessions have role plays for parents to experience what our children may experience/feel. Many of the parents and I found these quite helpful. For example, "what would it feel like to be told you have 'no right to feel that way?'"

The participants learn the philosophy including skills /techniques in a fun way. Each week there is an **Assignment** so that the parents can use these skills discussed in the session with their own children. In the beginning of the next session they share how it went. There is also assigned readings giving more information: Questions Most Often Asked in *How To Talk So Kids Will Listen and Listen So Kids Will Talk* by the authors and "Parents' Stories" in *How To Talk So Kids Will Listen* and *Listen So Kids Will Talk* and *Siblings Without Rivalry* which shares parents' experiences of how they put the new skills to use with their children. The participants are also asked to share one idea that spoke to them, found interesting or helpful or seemed important about the chapters they read weekly.

There is a **Reminder Card** for each session that summarizes the skills learned each week which parents can put on their refrigerators etc. so they can easily refer to them. At the last session **Reminder Cards** are reviewed together, discussing which ones specifically helped the parents.

I encourage the parents to take and use what resonates to them and make it suit their family. When you have a tool box filled with many tools, on your shoulder, then you can take out a skill to use with a particular child or incident which may not work with another child at another time. This is what my husband, Stu, reiterates during the workshop.

When something the parent needs to address is going on, I encourage the parents to stick with one item to talk about even if there are several issues going on at a time. Later on, one-by-one you can tackle other issues, perhaps by **Problem Solving.**

Parents, like their children during **Problem Solving,** have great ideas. For example, one parent suggested having a "**Problem Solving** Notebook" that the children could write down their ideas for the next **Problem** that needs to be solved and get to see again how they solved a past problem. (Thanks, Emily)

Another idea from a parent was separating the siblings during a **Problem Solving** time and individually get their feedback without the other sibling around or if it was between the parent and child, separate and write down ideas to bring back to solve a problem. (Thanks, Devyani)

Another parent used **Problem Solving** with her daughter and a friend. (Thanks, Anne)

I have been sharing this workshop with parents, moms to be, (once I had three pregnant Moms who sat together in the circle) grandparents, teachers, school counselors, leaders of camp counselors, therapists, etc. with very positive results. One of the most amazing combinations of people was when a mother and the stepmother attended so they would both be on the same page with raising the child.

I set up the participants in a circle. One suggestion from participants was for them to have tables in front of them for when they are writing.

Problem Solving: When people put their ideas into solving a problem, they are more invested into seeing it through. **Problem Solving** is time-consuming, but I believe well worth it. It can be used for making up family or school rules plus solving conflicts.

Role playing situations may help your child during difficult and other situations. Discuss problems and role play situations involving siblings, school, friends, what to do when you and a sibling, parent, friend disagree about what to play, bullying, etc. **Problem Solving** can also be used in *Family Meetings.* Please see **Chapter 3** for more information.

I have had a Mom and Dad alternate every other week (Thanks, Todd and Robin) and also the other parent attend the next time I gave the workshop. (Thanks, Margaret) One time I gave a morning class and an evening class the same day. I had one parent attend the day session and the other parent the night one. I have had grandparents attending with the parent and by themselves. One workshop I had five couples. It is truly amazing to have both parents on the same page and not to have a babysitting problem.

The following exercise I use to help adults realize it takes time to learn something new and to be patient with themselves while learning:

To learn something, it takes time. When you first begin to do something, it may feel "funny." Try this. Clasp your hands together and see which thumb is on the top. Now unclasp it and then clasp it again, this time with the opposite thumb on top. How does this feel? (strange, funny, odd, wrong, perhaps.) Now quickly claps and unclasp several times changing which thumb is on top. End with the second thumb on top. Now how does it feel? Perhaps, not so odd, not so bad. It is because you are getting used to it.

I believe that awareness is the first step in changing.

I also talk about muscles needing to be moved to work well.

To be proficient at something one needs to practice and persevere both for children and adults. For example, in learning to play an instrument, academics, sports, sewing, dance, etc. I suggest for the adult to think back to when they learned something new and how it takes time to become proficient. I also encourage parents to learn something new and see how difficult it can be in the beginning. This will aid them in being emphatic to their children and all they are learning.

"Every child needs to be seen as a multifaceted being, now shy and withdrawn, now boisterous and outgoing; now slow and thoughtful, now swift and purposeful; now stubborn and uncooperative, now flexible, But never the same, always in process, always with the capacity for change and growth." *How To Talk So Kids Can Learn at Home and in School* by Faber and Mazlish. page 212.

"Every child needs to be encouraged to experience the pleasures of sports, song, dance, theater and art without worrying about having to be the star athlete or a musical genius or the class actress or the family artist." *How To Talk So Kids Can Learn at Home and in School* by Faber and Mazlish. page 213.

"Talk to the situation not to the personality and character which is the cardinal rule of communication, the essence of effective communication." *Teacher and Child* by Dr. H. Ginott, page 71.

A parent shared these very interesting spiritual words at one of the *Parenting Communication Workshop, How To Talk So Kids will Listen™* by Adele Faber and Elaine Mazlish which I want to share with you, the reader. They seem quite relevant. "Listen to your heart, your truth," "Whatever you resist, persists," and the issue of karma: "What you give you will receive." (support) (Thanks, Dawn)

Parents have asked me should their older children read the Dr. Ginott and Faber/Mazlish books? I say great. They are books on *communication* and we can all work on our *communication* skills.

One parent shared with me that she had left out the *How To Talk So Kids Will Listen & Listen So Kids Will Talk* book and her mother had read a section of it and tried one of the skills which worked. The grandmother was amazed.

Another grandmother who was visiting her family attended a class. She shared with us that she had attended a class many years ago on the book, *How To Talk So Kids Will Listen & Listen So Kids Will Talk.* She was happy it was still being offered and how helpful it had been to her.

Many parents have told me that they would rather work during the six or seven weeks of the *Workshop* on one skill until they became comfortable with it and then try another. I think this is fine.

I also give out a paper to the participants to keep with background information about Faber and Mazlish studying with Dr. Ginott, and about my husband and me and Zelba Gross and Dr. Ginott.

I have a Notebook on Dr. Ginott and Faber and Mazlish with many articles which I have available for the participants.

Of course, having daycare for the children during the workshops would be very beneficial.

When we talk about descriptive praise, the authors stress the importance of when a child brings you something they have made or drawn, describe. Hold off saying what you think it is. Just describe. It may look like a flower to you but to the child it may be something else. One can also say, "Tell me about it."

Faber and Mazlish stress when we are *communicating* with others, look at the person, and do not multitask.

When one multitasks you may not be "There" for your child.

Two hour sessions seemed more beneficial for the weekly sessions than one and one half hour.

Some parents liked meeting every week, whereas some liked every other week giving them more time to work on the skills.

I had a play therapist speak to me about her beginning to chair the workshops in another state. She emailed me and then we spoke on the phone about it. (Thanks, Jennifer and Patricia)

Think how would you (the parent) feel in specific situation your children are in.

There is also a DVD program of these workshops but I choose to use the CDs.

Feedback

Comments from Participants of the Two *Parenting Communication Workshops, How To Talk So Kids Will Listen*™ and *Siblings Without Rivalry*™ both by Adele Faber and Elaine Mazlish.

"I observed Julienne being the chair person of the last program which was an integration and discussion of six previous weeks of skills. Julienne's enthusiasm, positive approach and ability to keep the group focused on the topic was exemplary. Afterward, many in the group expressed a desire to somehow continue so they formed a support group which met once a month at the library. Several parents spoke to me about how helpful the workshop was in improving communication with their children." (Supervisor) (Thank, Connie)

"The class was so helpful and inspiring to me and is causing sweet shifts in my relationships everywhere. I really enjoyed being in your delightful compassionate energy." (a participant)

"The participants told me they felt comfortable discussing their personal situations as you are approachable, honest, patient, and nonjudgmental. I admired how you humanized the sessions when you shared your own struggles you have had. You even personalized your relationship with each individual by listening to their needs, bringing materials you had or recommended books and techniques." (coordinator/contact/parent) (Thanks, Deyani)

"I really enjoyed attending the 'Siblings'™ class. It has helped to put my other children's feelings into perspective as they adjust to their new brother." (parent with a newly born third child)

"Due to your class, 'How To Talk So Kids'™ I have been able to more effectively communicate with my children and others which has improved our family life tremendously. I love that my children have even picked up on some of the techniques and are practicing them with each other." (a participant)

"I was very pleased with the meetings of *How To Talk.*™ I have seen a wonderful response from my children. I have been using the tips and techniques that I learned in the course. My husband will be taking the class next time it is offered. And I am looking forward to the *Siblings Without Rivalry workshop.*™" (a participant)

"My child was unhappy having to come in from playing outside to shower. She was very angry. I told her to tell the shower how she felt, After a few, I do not like you, Shower. I am going to run hot and cold water, Shower, her mood changed and she went on her way." (Thanks, Anne)

"The presentation style was a factor in making this workshop so good for me. It was a very relaxed atmosphere and so I felt secure sharing in the group. You did an outstanding job making us all feel comfortable. You made sure you followed up on any request or concerns for individual members of the classes. A "support" group dynamic formed quickly and you lovingly nurtured it." (a participant) Please check out later on in this **Chapter** for more information.

"This class has changed my household. I am able to talk to my children now." (a participant)

"Julienne Marks has been outstanding in presenting so much information in the time allowed in 'Siblings Without Rivalry.'™ Her energy and personality made it fun for all her students." (a grandparent)

"The skills and techniques I learned will definitely help me with my summer program, but I was not prepared for the far-reaching effect it had on my *communication* with my husband, grandchildren, friends, and coworkers. Your passion for the subject was apparent in every class, along with your thorough knowledge of communication skills making you an expert in your field. Your nonthreatening, always diplomatic manner made you a perfect facilitator for this program." (Summer Youth College Coordinator)

I had one patron who was attending when there was one of the horrendous school shootings, who said to me that day, "Why isn't this being presented everywhere? This workshop is really about peace." (a participant)

"It is heartwarming to see someone put their beliefs into action by sharing the, 'How To Talk'™ and 'Siblings. '™ Keep up the great work, lady!" (Thanks, Terry)

Julienne Marks

"Julienne has made a wonderful impact on our family. Her presentation of the '*How To Talk*'™ workshop was instrumental in the raising of our daughter. The lessons we have learned will be forever applied in this household and many of my friends' household. Words will not express thank you enough." (Thanks, Tammy)

The '*How To Talk*'™ you presented has helped me see parenting in a different light. The information that you imparted to the participants was truly inspirational. I needed what you had to offer at the right time. As you retire the community will truly miss your dedication and hard work you and your husband presented as a team for the welfare of children and their parents." (a participant)

"I made copies and put the reminder cards on construction paper and laminated them. I put them on a metal ring so I can share them with my husband, refer to it myself and even use it with my students." (a patron and Teacher) (Thanks, Bileni)

"Your passion for teaching the parenting *classes 'How To Talk*'™ and '*Siblings*'™ makes learning very interesting and exciting. It is so refreshing to see your enthusiasm for teaching this class and ensuring that parents have tools to have healthy, productive relationships with their children I have found the information to be very helpful for my family." (Thanks, Sheryl)

"I want to thank you for your competent teaching ability. You were always very well prepared and kept the class on task. (A participant)

"Mrs. Marks was a skilled and thoughtful facilitator. She was well organized and prepared. Each session was thorough, creative and presented with much enthusiasm." (a new parent and therapist)

"Julienne has an amazing grasp of the principles upon which her workshop is developed. She is able to apply them in a variety of very challenging situations asked by the participants of the group with real life answers, not straight from the text answers. Plus the workshop was fun." (a participant)

"You are an amazing teacher and so much of what you taught me has stuck with me and I have used through my parenting journey. I needed all of the wonderful Parenting Classes, 'How To Talk'™ and 'Siblings'™ that you taught." (Thanks, Liz)

I have also encouraged parents to come back and do the workshop again. I attached to the flyers the following: "If you have attended either *How To Talk So Kids Will Listen*™ or the *Siblings Without Rivalry*™ workshops previously, you are most welcome to attend again; this workshop can be beneficial both as a refresher and as a reinforcement, since you and your child are different ages and there have been changes in both of you. Plus sharing your stories with others can benefit all." Now, the participants would hear from parents who were using Dr. Ginott's humane philosophy and that it often worked. It wasn't only me "singing" the praises of Dr. Ginott's work. For example, "I can't believe how by just acknowledging my child's feelings, he calms down" or "We use **Problem Solving** all the time and yes it is time-consuming, but the children love to put in their ideas which are often tougher than us parents would suggest. We don't always follow all the steps but it works." or "One word works so well instead of speaking in paragraphs." (Said by both a parent of a four year old and a parent of a teenager, at the same class).

I had one parent come back five times and each time she said she received benefits out of the workshop, *'How To Talk'* ™ because both her child and herself were older and different things were happening in their lives. (Thanks, Laura)

One parent told me, "I needed reinforcement and I received it by attending the workshops 'How To Talk' ™ and Siblings Without Rivalry™ again and again." (Thanks, Anne)

Julienne Marks

While I was Working at a Library

I was telling a patron about the *Parenting Communication Workshop, How To Talk So Kids Will Listen™* by Adele Faber and Elaine Mazlish and I noticed another parent listening. When I was through explaining the workshop to the first parent, I asked the second patron if she wanted more information. She said her husband had taken the class. She told this to the first patron and to me how wonderful and helpful the workshop was for her family.

I was talking with a parent who had been in one of the *Parenting Communication Workshops, How To Talk So Kids Will Listen™* and *Siblings Without Rivalry™* both by Adele Faber and Elaine Mazlish. She had her 10-year-old son with her. She introduced me to him and he said his mom now listened to him. He said it twice. She actually shared this in the class also.

The two workshop kits, as well as, more information about the workshops including an Overview, Research Findings, Frequently Asked Questions, Feedback From Parents and Professionals, and Ask Adele and Elaine can be found on the following website. www.fabermazlish.com

I also shared/worked with and mentored two dynamic Moms (it was time to pass the torch) who began by taking the *Parenting Communication Workshops, How To Talk So Kids Will Listen™* and *Siblings Without Rivalry™* both by Adele Faber and Elaine Mazlish several times with me. I approached both of them and asked if they would be interested in becoming chairpersons. After we did the workshops together, they were ready to become chairpersons. What a great experience for me and I hope for them. Please note their comments. (Thanks Devvani and Anne)

I was asked by a former parent participant in these workshops to work with her doing the workshops. I had to refuse as I was working on this Book. (Thanks, Tuma)

Feedback

"With enormous patience, gentle reminders and your words of wisdom, these workshops have been a pleasure and exciting. Thank you for being my Mentor." (Thanks, Devyani, who is a parent, who wanted to become a Chairperson with the *Parenting Communication Workshops, How To Talk So Kids Will Listen ™* and *Siblings Without Rivalry™* both by Faber and Mazlish.

"Thank you, Julienne for being our Mentor. I have my daughter to thank for bringing you into our lives. (She loved your **Story Time**) Your feedback is very helpful and encouraging and I often find myself thinking, 'What would Julienne Do?' You are an inspiration. (Thanks, Anne, who is a parent and wanted to become a Chairperson with the *Parenting Communication Workshops, How To Talk So Kids Will Listen ™* and *Siblings Without Rivalry™* both by Faber and Mazlish)

Many parents with whom I have shared the *Parenting Communication Workshops, How To Talk So Kids Will Listen™* and *"Siblings Without Rivalry™* both by Faber and Mazlish would keep in touch.

While I was working, some parents were interested after the *Parenting Communication Workshops, How To Talk So Kids Will Listen™* and *Siblings Without Rivalry™* both by Faber and Mazlish were completed to continue to meet. They wanted more. We therefore formed a Parent Support Group. We would then continue to meet and talk about various parenting issues/topics. Sometimes we met at the library. One time the group met outside the library without me, since strong bonds had been formed. These new friendships seemed to happen frequently during the workshops and afterwards during the

Parent Support Group. Then after I retired, the Parent Support Group was held in my home once a month. except during the summer. This was a continuation of my mentoring.

Possibilities of what to discuss during a Parent Support Group could include

o   Individual problems or joys using skills learned
o   Decide on a topic the month before
o   Dr. Ginott's *Lessons.*
o   Themes such as unstructured play, holidays, summer, children being creative without the help from an adult, lying, no screen time, meltdowns, friends, read a Parenting book and discuss it, etc.

Feedback

"I really do love all of the ideas this group brings up and shares and thinking about the concepts and what's great is that we can agree or disagree, think it's great or think it's crazy, use it or not, pass it on or not, but I love pondering it all and figuring out what fits, or doesn't fit our individual family. Thank you for putting on this group so we can all bounce ideas off of each other. I love reflecting on parenting perspectives." (Thanks, Sarah)

"I really find our monthly meetings so refreshing and they bring so much value to my life. I could not ask for more. I appreciate the effort you make to change. I admire that about you. So much to learn from you. You are a wonderful role model. Thank you Stu and Julienne for opening your hearts and home." (Thanks, Deyani)

"I am so grateful I found you and this group! I am trying to be a better Mom and your notes really help." (Thanks, Paloma)

"The parents are so lucky to have you as their awesome support." (A therapist who attended) (Thanks, Pat)

"Thank you for starting and maintaining a parenting revolution. You are best leader for this in the County. I love how caring and involved you stay in anything you do. Thank you for working so hard to make this world a better place for all." (Thanks, Lee)

"We are so lucky to have you guiding us as we figure out this parenting thing." (Thanks, Anne)

"You have all helped me soooo much - I am happy to have found this safe community in which to share." (Thanks, Jayashree)

I also have given several general talks about Parenting, at a Family Retreat at a Hindu Temple, a branch of a Public Library, and a Mom's group.

Feedback

"The highlight was your causal talk to the adults based on Dr. Ginott's philosophy." (Thanks Devyani, contact at Hindu Temple)

"The parents who attended benefited greatly from your parenting tips and words of encouragement. Two mothers registered for your *Parenting workshop, 'How To Talk'™* by Faber and Mazlish (Thanks Sarah, President of Mom's Group)

Another Parenting Aid - Nonviolent Communication
Nonviolent Communication (NVS) by Dr. Marshall Rosenberg. There are free tip series which I am finding quite helpful: *Living Compassion NVC Tip Series, Compassionate Educator NVC Tip Series*, and *Compassionate Parenting NVC Tip Series.*

Nonviolent Communication Parenting and Family Communication Books:
Respectful Parents Respectful Kids: 7 Keys to Turn Family Conflict Into Cooperation by Hart and Hodson

Parenting From Your Heart: Sharing the Gifts of Compassion, Connection and Choice by Kashtan
Raising Children Compassionately: Parenting the Nonviolent Way by Rosenberg
    A book I just began as I was finalizing this Book is *The Collapse of Parenting: How We Hurt Our Kids When We Treat Them Like Grown-Ups, The Three Things You Must Do To Help Your Child or Teen Become a Fulfilled Adult.* by Dr. Sax. I am finding it an interesting read.

MY PERSONAL LIFE

    I am married to Stu who is a dentist since 1969 and we have one lovely daughter, Elissa born in 1978. I was very lucky that I could stay home in her formative years. I would very occasionally work outside the home doing workshops. Elissa is a high school drama director and over the course of the past twelve years has put on many meaningful productions. As part of a Slam Poetry lesson, one of her drama classes wrote an original piece entitled "Scared" which really moved me to tears. My precious grandson, Ethan Benjamin who was born in 2006, took his first steps on the stage and he loves acting, sports, dancing, singing, science, robotics, and reading. He calls me "Ma." Please check out in **Chapter Five** under Family Stories to find out why. I am one of 4 siblings, my older brother Bill, and my younger twin sisters, Marlene, and Marsha. It is interesting we all have become teachers at some point of each of our lives. I have a cousin who was like a sister to me while growing up, Jo-Ann. My family has been very supportive of me over the years and I am eternally grateful.

    I grew up in New York on Long Island and moved to Florida in 1983 to be near one of my sisters and then to Georgia in 2008 to be with my daughter and grandson. I have a cat named Peaches, whom I adopted while in Georgia. She is my third cat. In the past I have collected dolls. I love to dance. I have taken ballet, (my favorite) belly dancing, Zumba and yoga classes. A friend once said to me, "Ballet and Zumba are like fire and ice - total opposites. Isn't it nice to be able to choose what one wants to do?" (Thanks, Mae) I enjoy plays, museums, especially history and children's, classical music, (I adore Barbra Streisand) dance, animals, children's literature, and nature. I enjoy learning about the Native American culture. I enjoy food from other places especially Indian cuisine. Peace Education, Multiculturalism, self-expression, doing for others, and kindness are all important concepts I have striven for throughout my life.

I have found the following books and/or websites helpful.

http://thinkexist.com/quotation/i_am_only_one-but_still_i_am_one-i_cannot_do/10674.html and
http://www.beliefnet.com/Quotes/Inspiration/H/Helen-Keller/I-Am-Only-One-But-I-Am-Still-One-I-Cannot-Do-Eve.aspx
Hale thinkexist.com/quotation/i_am_only_one-but_i_am_one-I
www.brainyquote.com/quotes/quotes/e/edwardever393297.html
Lama http://www.goodreads.com/quotes/34322-this-is-my-simple-religion-no-need-for-temples-no
www.fabermazlish.com
http://www.goodreads.com/quotes/48-three-things-in-human-life-are-important-the-first-is
http://www.imdb.com/title/tt0034492/quotes
http://thinkexist.com/quotation/you_see_things-and_you_say--why-but_i_dream/13471.html and
https://www.google.com/search?q=shaw+you+see+things+and+you+say+why&ie=utf-8&
http://www.ctvnews.ca/world/emotional-moment-elephant-cries-tears-of-joy-as-it-walks-free-after-50-years-1.1908004
www.peta.org

http://go.networksuperstars.net/2009/03/march-2009-casey-cebulski-city-of-lakes.htlm
www.perpetualkid.com/blackmail-postcards.html
www.petakids.com
www.betweenparentandchild.com./index.php?s=content&p=H
aim
http://www.metrolyrics.com/love-is-the-answer-lyrics-todd-rundgren.html
http://www.nonviolentcommunication.com/
https://youtu.be/6gUhbaECFH0
http://www.healyourlife.com/blogs/louise-hay-blog/mistakes-far-okay

Chapter 3

FAMILY

QUOTATIONS

"Children are like wet cement. Whatever falls on them makes an impression." Dr. Haim Ginott, *Between Parent and Child.* (Child psychologist and Holocaust Survivor)

"There are only two lasting bequests we can give our children. One is roots. The other is wings." Hodding Carter, Jr.

"Family are like branches on a tree, we all grow in different directions, yet our roots remain as one." Potpourrigift.com.

"Kids spell love T-I-M-E." John Crudel

"Your children are not your children. They are the sons and daughters of Life's longing for itself. They come through you but not from you. And though they are with you yet they belong not to you." Kahlil Gibran

"It is easier to build strong children than repair broken men." Frederick Douglas

"If children live with criticism, they learn to condemn." Dr. Dorothy Law Nolte

"The solution to adult problems tomorrow depends on a large measure upon how our children grow up today." Margaret Mead.

"If a child is to keep his inborn sense of wonder, he needs the companionship of at least one adult who can share it, rediscovering with him the joy, excitement, and mystery of the world we live in." Rachel Carson

"I sincerely believe that for the child, and for the parent seeking to guide him, it is not half so important to know as to feel. If facts are the seeds that later produce knowledge and wisdom, then the emotions and the impressions of the senses are the fertile soil in which the seeds must grow. The years of early children are the time to prepare the soil." Rachel Carson

A Sense of Wonder, "Play, Incorporating Animistic and Magical Thinking Is Important Because It: Fosters the healthy, creative and emotional growth of a child. Forms the best foundation for later intellectual growth. Provides a way in which children get to know the world and creates possibilities for different ways of responding to it. Fosters empathy and wonder." Rachel Carson

"Parents don't come full bloom at the birth of the first baby. In fact, parenting is about growing. It's about our own growing as much as it is about our children's growing and that kind of growing happens little by little." Fred Rogers

GENERAL INFORMATION ABOUT THE AUTHOR, FAMILIES AND PARENTING

Before I decided that I wanted to become a parent, I did quite a lot of thinking about parenting. I read books, took classes, and talked to parents and grandparents. For many years, I have been involved with parents through my jobs as a: teacher, camp counselor and camp administrator, youth advisor, museum educator, peace educator, librarian, and Chairperson of *Parenting Communication Workshops, How To Talk So Kids Will Listen* ™ and *Siblings Without Rivalry*™ by both Faber and Mazlish. When my daughter was young I attended many

"Mommy and Me" programs where I met other Moms and talked and listened to them and the facilitator while my daughter would play with the other children. I was lucky that I could be home with my daughter while she was growing up. I will be sharing some of my experiences as a parent.

My husband became involved with "Daddy and Me" programs, as well as "Indian Princess" sponsored by the YMCA. He chose to be on the Boards of the YMCA, two *Waldorf Schools*, and on committees at our daughter's school so he could make a difference. He also became quite involved in the afterschool theater program my daughter was involved with, taking her and helping to build sets, even going on Theater conventions. He also took her clothes shopping, something I disliked.

I recently saw something beautiful. Sitting across from my husband and me, a father and his young daughter were out to eat together. The Dad was asking her about her day and how he liked what she was wearing. She was coloring the restaurant's children's menu. I could see she had a bag of things to do also. Such a wonderful thing to see!

I will be sharing some ideas, philosophy, and communication *programs* that I have presented through the years to families. I will also be sharing some "Family Rituals" and "Rites of Passage."

When I shared some of these with parents, many told me it began them thinking of ideas that would work for them in their homes, which is one of my goals of this Book.

I believe that it is up to the parents to share with their family their ideas, as well as to elicit from their children, on how the family will work, how important kindness will be, how everyone treats each other, and how helpful they are to each other and others. You, as the parent, decide on your Family's lifestyle choices. Think about what values you want to instill in your child. What type of home environment do you want to have?

Julienne Marks

Before I became a Librarian, I made up and sold "Informal Bibliographies" to parents. I called them "Listings" on different topics such as Peace Education, Nature (Environment), Children Dealing with Death, Challenged Individuals, Cultures, Older People, Native American Indians, Only Children, Homeschooling, Animal Rights, Children's Magazines, Museums and Children, Feelings, Self-esteem/Self-concept, The Holocaust, Competition/Cooperation, TV, Your Family Tree (Genealogy), Moving, Conflict Resolution, etc. As I look back at this list, I am amazed of how many of them have been major topics/themes in bibliographies I had asked library staff to prepare. I am also realizing that these themes are ones that are important to me. What topics are important to you? You may want to put them in your *programs*!

I believe it is very important to be kind and understanding to mothers and to ask if you can help if a Mom or Dad seems to need it. For example, on a plane playing peek-a-boo, waving, or smiling to give that parent a much needed minute or two.

I was at a tire place and it was so amazing how a nursing mom and a two-year-old kept the *connection*. Later she told me she has two more children at home that were in school!

FAMILY PROGRAMS/ACTIVITIES I HAVE SHARED
Family Connection Time

I wanted to offer a workshop both for families to interact alone as a family, as well as to *connect* with other families by participating in some activities in a group. My goal in having this *program* was to have a time for families to reconnect minus the world's many outside influences. There were games and projects for each family and many activities for all families to do together. Some examples: playing cooperative games, sharing books, making something as a family, talking and listening, telling stories, having fun, singing, making memories, etc. which were all part of this "Family Connection Time." I had been asked several times to share this program again and more frequently. Besides being given in a library setting, I did this type of program at a YMCA and a synagogue.

A Sample of **PR (Public Relations)**
for "Family Connection Time"

Make some memories by spending time with your family at the library! Bring all or some of your family members. There will be games and projects for each family and activities for all families to do together! The activities are geared for school age children, but all ages are welcome. Children must be accompanied by an adult. Registration required. Approx. 45 minutes (usually in the evening or on a Saturday).

A Sample of an **Agenda** for "Family Connection Time" Please see the **Agenda** below that each family received on entering the room for more specifics about the program. Parents were encouraged to turn off their phones during this program.

I asked all families to join the opening activity, Ice Breaker #1, Being an Audience #7, and the closing activity of Music #8. For the balance of the time, families may choose to do any or all of #2-6 in any order according to their family's needs. Find an *area* in the room that will be for your individual family. If you want to present #2, please prepare that first.

1. Ice Breaker: Machine

All Families Together

We will be making up a new kind of machine. One family begins by making a sound and coming up with a movement that is part of the machine. The first family repeats their sound and the movement as if the machine is running. Then another family stands by or *connects* to the first family and

51

creates their own movement and sound. When all the families are *connected*, the machine will go faster and faster until it is going so fast that it breaks down, with all of the parts of the machine collapsing. Then everyone gently falls to the floor. *On Stage: Theatre Games and Activities for Kids* by Lisa Bany-Winters, page 40.

Individual Families

2. Paper Bag Dramatics

A variety of props will be placed in large bags. Choose one for your family. Your family will then make up a short story/skit/play incorporating the props. If you would like, you can use the props differently than they are "really" used for. At the end of the session, if you like, your family may present it to the other families. Check out My Book, *Education in Different Environments,* under Libraries for a sample **Agenda** of "Paper Bag Dramatics."

3. Complimenting Time

Each person gets complimented by each family member. You may want to have the person being complimented in the center of a circle. One suggestion would be to stay away from physical appearance and use, for example, character traits such as helping, being kind, etc. Some families like to write the compliments down so that the family member may look at it at other times. Please see *Siblings Without Rivalry* by Faber and Mazlish page 143 and "An Unforgettable Classroom Exercise" for examples of how helpful this can be. Please check out in this **Chapter** under *Family Meetings* for more information.

4.   Favorite Books

Talk about your favorite books and listen to the ones your family members like.

5.   Family Ritual

Talk about beginning a new "Family Ritual" you would like to implement for your family. It could be for mealtimes, bedtime, holidays, etc. Include the ideas of the children. Please see in this **Chapter** under "Family Rituals."

6.   Choose Poems to Read

Choose poems and read aloud to your family from the Poetry Notebook (a collection of poems from *Highlights Magazine*, etc.). When you have finished with the poems, please return them where you picked them up so that others can read them also.

All Families Together

7.   Being Actors or an Audience

Present your "Paper Bag Dramatics" story/skit/play to the other families.

8.   Music

  a. Let us move our bodies to *The William Tell Overture* by Gioachino Rossini
  b. Up Activity: *Hokey Pokey*

Julienne Marks

c. Sing Alongs: *She'll Be Coming Round the Mountain* and *Make New Friends and Keep the Old.*

9. (If given at a library): Books on Families would be available to be taken out.

Other possibilities of additions to the **Agenda**: Collage making of your family's interests (having appropriate magazines available to cut up), act out pantomimes, orally add to a story, make a shield or poster representing your family, with words or pictures, such as "We do ....for fun, We do ....for love, (filling in after "We do...") or add your own ideas, etc.

Feedback

"It was wonderful to be able to focus on my family during this *program*. I learned some interesting things about my daughter. For example, she enjoys performing in front of others." (parent)

"I liked having my parents concentrating on the family with no interruptions from their phones. My parents are actually fun." (older child)

"My family enjoyed the Machine Game and making the collage. Thank you for offering this. My husband and I are also taking the *Parenting Communication Workshop,* 'How To Talk So Kids '™. It is wonderful. You are a great teacher." (parent)

This was a very successful program. Many parents and children favorably commented orally that they wanted it longer and again.

Family Nights

Family Nights (or *Family Days*) are special regular set aside times (can be weekly, monthly, etc.) that the family spends together. It can be structured following the same format, a template all the time: for example can begin with a prayer, the sharing of individual or family news, compliment-ing time, talking and listening, (discussions) sharing of an ac-tivity (for example cooking together), playing board games, role playing situations that might happen to children (for ex-ample, what would you do if your neighbor next door was get-ting bullied?), making a craft, doing something fun, going someplace together (museum, park, favorite place, etc.), cele-brating or learning about one's religious holidays or others, sharing your values through stories, etc., ending with a snack or song, or it can be unstructured/spontaneous/flexible about what things to do. My family of origin had on Fridays, *Family Nights*. One thing we would do is watch classic movies and talk about them. My brother's love of classic movies probably began there. (Thanks, Bill)

What would work for your family (contents, how long, when, how often) depends on the ages and temperaments of the children. And as the children grow, this will change.

In the following if geared to a particular religion one can change that orientation to be relevant to your family. Book-lets: *Love Happens in Families* by Castovnova, etc. *Family Nights Summer Vacation and Family Nights Throughout the Year* by Reilly, Abby Press, *Empowering Families and Family Days* by Lechner, National Marriage Encounter, *Together Time* by Meltz, *Sun Sentinel* May 18, 2003 C., *Family Fun Nights* by Cynthia Copeland.

Family Meetings

The goals here are to brainstorm or **Problem Solve** conflicts, plus build up/*connect* the family. **Problem Solving/** brainstorming is when people including children put their thoughts into solving a problem, and then everyone feels more invested into seeing it through. Bringing the child into discus-sing what to do about problems, thus eliciting from the children their possible solutions, their feedback, and listening to his/her ideas, helps them to be more interested in solving the problem. When one has used some of their ideas, it is quite validating to the child. A parent used the term "buy in" when a child puts his/her suggestions into solving a problem. (Thanks, Emily) Using this approach is time consuming, but I think, well worth it. We used it with my daughter and grandson.

Family Meetings can be used for making up family rules and can also be a time to role-play.

This can be a good place to discuss problems involving siblings, bullying, school, friends, what to do when you and a friend disagree about what to play, etc. For example, the advantages and disadvantages of playing alone vs. with others.

I believe that teamwork needs to be experienced within a family and can be part of *Family Nights*. For example, stating, we are a family and in our family we all help with the house's chores since our family is a team. One may need to say repeatedly that in our family we bring each other up, not down. Games may help to have a strong family *connection*. For more ideas please see *Family Team Building Games* by Miller.

One suggestion would be that during both *Family Nights* and *Family Meetings* to turn off all technology and therefore one can fully concentrate/focus on having fun or solving individual or family problems.

Please also see the books, *Between Parent and Child by* Dr. H. Ginott, *How To Talk So Kids Will Listen* And *Listen So Kids Will Talk,* and *Siblings Without Rivalry* by Adele Faber and Elaine Mazlish, and *Positive Discipline* by Jane Nelsen for more information about *Family Meetings.*

Family Ritual

Children enjoy traditions and **Family Rituals.** It strengthens a child's sense of belonging and security. Routine is also important in a child's life. Rituals add to that need. For more information please see *The Importance* of *Family Rituals* by Tsh Oxenredier, 2009

Families can have their own Rituals or often grandparents share Rituals that have been going on for years. Make up your own Rituals (customs, practice, traditions, and memories) as a family and continue it year by year. Who knows, your children might continue them. It may be a special prayer or blessing before or after meals or when you wake up or go to sleep. It could be a coming-of-age passage or ceremony for teen boys and girls. It may be the way you celebrate holidays.

A parent in my support group shared how she wants to make family memories and she is doing it. For example, on Fridays when her preschoolers do not have school, she wants the day to be relaxing with no schedule on when to eat, nap, go places, etc. I think this is quite important. (Thanks, Sarah)

For example, during the Christmas season, every year, my daughter and I went to see the Nutcracker Ballet. Prior to the ballet, we would listen to the magnificent music by T. Pyotr Ilyich Tchaikovsky and read some of the books on the Nutcracker. Two favorites, due to the illustrations, are Mary Engelbreit's *Nutcracker* and the *Nutcracker* by Susan Jeffers.

When my daughter was young, I would have teenagers come to my home with me still working in another part of the house. The teen and my daughter would play. As I had many teens who wanted to do this, each teen would have something special she would do with my daughter, as dress up, work on clay, read, etc. Both my young daughter and the teen seemed to benefit from this time together.

My grandson and I would go to the library once a week to pick out books. After my grandson would read a book or see a movie, he would want to make a costume of one of the characters with his Papa (grandfather) or me usually using large boxes. We have made a spaceship, an astronaut's outfit, a bee, dinosaur cave, etc.

My husband and I have put together photographs of us with our daughter plus my daughter and grandson together doing similar things. For example, when my husband had his Bar Mitzvah he was holding a special book and so was my daughter, my daughter and I both at Sixteen, at graduations, my daughter and my grandson sleeping around the same age, using a microphone, planting a garden, etc. These photographs side by side show the *connection* between family members.

When my daughter was quite young we began showing her photographs of her doing things, (being read to, having a bath, brushing her teeth, etc.) with us, her grandparents, my siblings, and key people in her life. We would talk about them and show her the pictures. My siblings would send letters, postcards, photos, and gifts to keep them known to my daughter and grandson. (Thank you Bill, Marsha, and Marlene.) Uncles and aunts can be so supportive and helpful in the journey of raising a child. Please note Melanie Notkin, the author of the book *Savvy Auntie: The Ultimate Guide for Cool Aunts, Great-Aunts, Godmothers, and All Women Who Love Kids*. She is also the founder of SavvyAuntie.com. "The more aunts and uncles the child has, the more influences a child has. If the uncle is a fantastic artist, the child may be inspired by that talent." And to be an aunt or uncle one doesn't need to be related.

Besides the mothers and fathers, the entire community was responsible for raising the Lakota child. The uncles and aunts also had parental duties especially the aunts on the mothers' side and the uncles on the fathers' side.

When my daughter was young we went on several Jewish weekends away with other families:

- One was with the 92nd Street Y(weekend)
- The Summer Institute of the National Havurah Committee in Philadelphia for a week
- Marriage Encounter Family Weekend

My daughter and husband enjoyed cruising which we did when my daughter was growing up. We went on a family cruise and some highlights for my grandson, Ethan was kissing a dolphin, going on a jet ski, playing giant chess with my husband, as well as, winning a dance contest at the Camp on the cruise ship.

Children want us. One way to acknowledge this is making time for memorable moments to do together. *Make Memories With Your Kids* by Goodwyn.

Here are some other books that might be beneficial:

- *The Book of New Family Traditions: How to Create Great Rituals for Holidays and Every Day* by Meg Cox
- *Not So Fast: Slow Down Solutions for Frenzied Families* by Kroeker.
- *Let's Make a Memory* by Gloria Gaither and Shirley Dobson
- *Prime Time Together With Kids* by Donna Erickson (Discovery Toys)
- *Kids and Weekends! Creative Ways to Make Special Days* by Hart and Mantell
- *The Big Book of Family Fun* by Ellis
- *The Alternative Celebrations Catalogue* by Shannon-Thornberry

A great family activity would be to make a Family Time Capsule filled with memories and treasures about your family. What a wonderful idea! *Preserve Memories: Create a Family Time Capsule.*

In *Atlanta Parent* May 2015, please check out *Savor the Moments* especially under *Mark Rites of Passage.* page 13.

In *Atlanta Parent*, January 2015, please check out *Family Traditions for the New Year* for ideas for each month "to help families strengthen bonds and make treasured memories," pages 16-17.

Julienne Marks

A friend shared with me the following idea. A "Memory Jar" which is filling a glass mason jar with small written pieces of paper with memories and dates. For example, a visit with someone, a grandchild's great day, a death of a friend, etc. One could look at these memories whenever one wanted to. A child and/or the parent could do this. (Thanks, Gretta)

Two meaningful songs I want to share about wishes parents may want for their children: *Forever Young* by Bob Dylan and *I Hope You Dance* sung by Lee Ann Womack.

Rites of Passage

A "Rite of Passage" gives one a chance to move up to a higher level of human social and educational development.

When I first began writing about "meaningful" "Rites of Passage" for coming of age (for example, when a young woman gets her menses), and for adults at different pivotal ages, I didn't know that there were many to learn about. I found *The Clear Red Stone: A Myth and the Meaning of Menstruation* by Kollmeyer and *First Moon Rising, The Making of a Menarche Ritual* by Soster-Olmer, *Mothering,* March 2010. The latter has some great ideas and resources. As I researched this topic, I found more and more people were celebrating "Rites of Passages."

Here are some other examples of "Rites of Passage" that my daughter was involved with. Some may not be considered "Rites of Passage" but part of growing. I included these here also.

In today's society, ceremonies, which have always been an important part of Scouting, continues to be. For example, becoming an Eagles Scout is quite an accomplishment.

Please see this **Chapter** about my daughter and husband being involved in Indian Princess.

Once a month my daughter and my husband, who were part of the Indian Princess program, attended meetings at different homes doing an activity and having a snack. They also went on campouts. It was a special time for them. They would talk and plan for the campouts for weeks before.

Breaking The Arrow Ceremonies were held at the big bonfire during a campout. During the Induction Ceremony new princesses were welcomed by the Nation Chief. During the Breaking Arrow Ceremony, older girls finding themselves busy with life as a young teenager, would say goodbye to the program hopefully following the life lessons experienced with their father during their years in the program. My daughter broke her arrow and I have it framed. She then helped the younger girls in her tribe and then it was time for her to move on.

For my daughter's Bat Mitzvah we went to Israel where she became a Bat Mitzvah on Mount Masada. I was so lucky to have my Mom and Uncle (my Father's brother) who looked like my Dad, also attending. (Thanks, Rabbi Skiddell.) We had been telling her that this was what we were going to do for her Bat Mitzvah from since she was very young. We also had a small party for her friends and family back in the States after her Bat Mitzvah at our synagogue. The gifts to the preteen guests were trees planted in Israel and the name of a pen pal from Israel that they could correspond with. As our daughter was dancing at this time, she and her dance teacher choreographed a dance called "Growing Up" which she performed to Whitney Huston's, *Greatest Love of All*. (Thanks, Linda) The dance was amazing! She also symbolically shared her Bat Mitzvah with someone from Ethiopia who had been denied the freedom to celebrate her Jewish heritage. This was so interesting. Her name was Esther which was my mother's name and whom Ethan, my grandson is named after.

When my daughter was in ninth grade she went with her class on an *Outward Bound* trip to the Everglades by canoes for four days. She learned through teamwork with her classmates how to deal with insects, navigating, rain, cooking, bathrooms, surviving in the wilderness, and *communicating.* The teens were left alone some of the time. During this trip, my daughter said she learned some interesting things about herself. It was quite an experience for her.

When my daughter was in High School, she took an amazing class called *Facing History, Facing Ourselves.* She felt it was one of the most important classes she took. *Facing History, Facing Ourselves* began as a history class about the ideas and events that led to the Holocaust, but soon involved much more.

My daughter also played Anne Frank in the play, *The Diary of Anne Frank,* where my husband played her father. How moving this was. She also sang some of the songs from the musical, *Yours, Anne* at another event. This was one of her favorite plays to be involved in as it combined her love of acting and her heritage. Plus she was quite knowledgeable about Anne Frank as in fifth grade she had done an extensive report on her.

When my daughter was in High School she attended once a week for several months a study period with others in preparation to go one week to Poland and one week to Israel on the *March of the Living.* It was a life changing event for her. She now understood why Israel was established. She also questioned how one human being could be so horrible to another human being.

My daughter was so affected by the *March of the Living* that her Master Thesis in the Interdisciplinary Arts from Nova Southeastern, was on how, by using Theatre, one can help the audience and players become more emphatic and compassionate. She put on twice, in a public school and at a Catholic School, the play, *I Never Saw Another Butterfly: Children's Drawings and Poems from the Terezin Concentration Camp,* 1942-1944 by Hana Volavkova (Editor). The effect on these teens was amazing to see and hear when they spoke about how the play affected them. As part of her Masters she also went over the summer to Sweden to direct teens in shows made up of international teens. She was part of the Lovewell Institute.

My daughter loved performing in theatres. Most of her after-school activities and her camping experiences were at at a local Children's Theater. She was also a drama camp counselor there. (Thank you, Janet and Darlene.) My daughter also attended a Fine Arts Sleep Away Camp. She danced with an extremely creative teacher who had her students perform at different venues. (Thanks, Linda)

One summer my daughter traveled around the country visiting different historical sites and attractions. She had a blast. She attended a reunion with some of the participants.

Quinceañera (feminine form of 'fifteen-year-old') is a celebration of a girl's fifteenth birthday in parts of Latin America and elsewhere in communities of people from Latin America. This birthday is celebrated differently from any other as it marks the transition from childhood to young womanhood.

I was told about a "Ritual" that a friend's young daughter had when she received her menses at age nine. Her Mom arranged for her to go out for lunch with an adult friend who also received her menses at a young age. They talked about the pluses and minuses about having the signs of puberty earlier than most of her peers. The Mom's Elder had a ceremony for her daughter sharing the Blood Mysteries; that having your period was powerful and beautiful and she also shared other empowering information about Women. The Elder also gave her a blessing tying the daughter into Women's Lineage, that she is now part of/on the path of a large Women's Group. (Thanks, Elaine and your daughter)

I was also told about when a friend's son became 13 and he studied with a Mentor about the importance of the "Rite of Passage," the transition from one stage (child) to being a young adult while still holding onto some aspects of both. He, his mentor, and Dad went to a mountain where they made a fire and offered up some items from his childhood, honoring where he had come from. Then he went off by himself for a vision quest. There was drumming and talk about the responsibilities of being a good man and the importance of being kind to women. He was given a beautiful knife. (Thanks, Elaine and your son)

I was talking to a friend whose children attend a *Waldorf School* and she shared with me that the fifth graders, at the end of the school year, participate in the Greek Olympiad with other regional *Waldorf Schools*. Please see My Book on *Education in Different Environments,* for more information on the *Waldorf School.*

I talked with the person in charge of this event at the *Waldorf School* I volunteer at, who explained the significance of this event in the fifth graders' lives. The children are saying goodbye to the baby years and honoring the coming of the teenage years. Also each event is a metaphor for life.

My daughter lost her first tooth after eating an apple (we later called it "the apple tooth") and since my husband is a dentist we went to his office and she was his first patient after lunch. It was very significant for us all. I told a grandparent this story about it being an "apple tooth." Her granddaughter lost her first tooth after eating a pancake. My friend loved my daughter's apple story. She told her daughter and now they refer to the lost tooth as "the pancake tooth." (Thanks, Mae) See how things can continue!

I know we all have tooth stories to share. *Throw Your Tooth on the Roof: Tooth Traditions from Around the World* is a very interesting book by Selby B. Beelerup.

I think these above events are so important in the lives of our children.

Many Pebbles to Make a Difference

Some books

- *Celebrating; Nurturing and Empowering Our Daugters* by Virginia Beane Rutter
- *From Boys to Men: Spiritual Rites of Passage in an Indulgent Age* by Bret Stephenson
- *The Wonder of Boys and The Wonder of Girls* by Michael Gurian

What is Walkabout?

At age 16, aborigines in the Australian outback do a Walkabout. It is a time to be tested under real life conditions and to realize he is responsible for the consequences. When the Walkabout is completed he would have demonstrated to himself and members of his community that he is ready to accept the responsibilities of being an adult.

At the Graham School there is an educational program designed for twelfth graders who wish to continue to grow outside the traditional classroom setting.

Sharing the Growth of Your Child

Take a photograph each year of your child in a large chair thus seeing their growth. We did this for both my daughter and now for my grandson using a large throne chair. This idea I took from "Life Magazine" or "Look Magazine" and seeing a child in a mother's full body bathing suit growing into it each year. We have the photographs hanging next to the chair. Think of your own item that would show the yearly growth of your child. People really enjoy seeing these photographs.

Here's another idea. Check out *Father And Son Take The Same Photo Every Year For 30 Years* by Jason Owen, September 17, 2015.

Julienne Marks

My Daughter in the chair

My Grandson in the chair

Celebration of Your Child's Birthday

Write in a Birthday Journal a letter to your child about the past year's activities and changes you have noticed. My father would sometimes write me a birthday letter in his handwriting and I treasure them.

And/or the parent is the interviewer who asks the child questions about the previous year. Record the interview with your voices. Children love to hear their sweet young voices as they mature. My daughter would say to me, "Is that really me?

Have a home party with a scavenger hunt, making a collage, doing "Paper Bag Dramatics" (See My Book on *Education in Different Environments,* under Libraries), Sing Traditional Songs. For example, depending on the age: *Farmer in the Dell, Here We Go Loopy Loo, All Around the Mulberry Bush, Hokey Pokey,* etc. Give something meaningful as a gift to the children like a book instead of a goody bag full of candy, etc.

One Birthday year we hired a Story Teller who told stories from different places. The invitation was in the shape of a passport. The children could come dressed in a costume from a different place. Their gifts were names of pen pals from other countries. The party was held at a Mexican restaurant. We gave the children a handmade passport and they could check off in their passports, which places the Story Teller told stories from. The Story Teller had a globe and would point to the place where her stories came from. (Thanks, Molly)

Talk about how in other cultures or countries birthdays are celebrated. A book about this is *Birthdays Around the World* by May Lankford and Karen Dager.

Instead of gifts, parents can give experiences for example attending concerts, plays, dance, hearing people talk about their passions, field trips to museums, etc. My daughter did this for my grandson. The entire family enjoyed it.

An example of a gift that can last for a year are magazine subscriptions of an interest of your child. Go online to find the many magazines that are available. For example, my grandson enjoys *Dig Into History* (Archaeology and Paleontology), *Cobblestone* (American History), and *Odyssey* (Science) all by *Cricket Magazines.*

Of course, books are also great gifts for any occasion, perhaps one a year of a *Series.* For example The *Illustrated Junior Library* series which has beautiful pictures of the Classics. Giving a book that is part of a *Series* shares a *connection* each year.

Encourage your birthday child to give a favorite or a new toy or money to children who are less fortunate than them and have fewer "things." (During Christmas read *The Littlest Angel* by Charles Tazewell.)

There are some websites at the end of this **Chapter** to encourage your child to give some of their birthday or winter holiday gifts to others now in need.

Isn't this wonderful? An 11 year old asked for teddy bears on her birthday which she donated to a local police department to give to children who needed a pick me up.

Give a gift that helps someone or an animal. By helping someone or an animal out, a child can learn about giving.

My daughter always loved animals. For her Bat Mitzvah "service" she gave some of her gift money to animals in Israel, as well as, visited a nursing home with an adult friend. My daughter adopted a whale and a manatee and my grandson adopted a dolphin. These were positive experiences due to having the children learning about that animal plus they were helping animals.

Volunteering as a Family to Help Others

"The best way to instill a commitment to service is to start at home. Encouraging small acts of kindness, like helping a family member who has had a rough day or caring for a pet, can teach even the smallest children the power of caring. As children grow, you can help them develop empathy and support good causes."

I really liked what Fred Rogers said that at one time or another all of us may need help. Please check out the book *Peaceable Neighbor: Discovering the Countercultural Mister Rogers* by Long, page 111

"We are all here on earth to help others" by Auden.

"Remember, if you ever need a helping hand, it's at the end of your arm, as you get older, remember you have another hand: The first is to help yourself, the second is to help others" by Audrey Hepburn.

Giving to someone who may really need the basics to Volunteering as a Family to Help Others is all part of giving. A weekly/monthly (steward) service for the community as a family or individually can help your family meet others' needs in different economic situations.

I believe that helping others is one reason we are on earth.

Start at home to foster a commitment to service to others or stewardship.

"Service is the rent we pay to be living. It is the very purpose of life and not something you do in your spare time." by Marian Wright Edelman

9 Ways to Teach Your Kids About Love Without a Word by Schroeder, *The Good Men Project.*

Moral: "No act of kindness, no matter how small is ever wasted." *The Lion and the Mouse, Aesop's Fables*

The Giving Family, Raising Our Children to Help Others by Price is another resource.

Encourage your child (or students) to pick a social issue that speaks or resonates with them. Have them read about it, talk to other interested people, find out about organizations that are helping in some way, etc. Encourage them to begin to help out. For example, helping animals or helping other children in other places who need help. There are many examples of children helping their community or others. Please see below for several examples.

'Kids and Smiles' was begun by an eight-year old whose goal was to bring smiles to children in hospitals by delivering smiles, toys cards and other prepared crafts.

5 year Old's Touching Act of Kindness Toward Homeless Man by O'Neil

Busy Kids Take Time to Help Others

Children Helping Children, Little Hands little Love, Youth United

In Atlanta, for example, *Family Service Saturdays* is Hands On Atlanta's newest volunteer program designed especially for families with children ages 5-12

Please check out this website which has some articles and resources to get your children involved in community service, volunteering, and starting to do good deeds on the behalf of less fortunate children and individuals.

http://www.artistshelpingchildren.org/get kidsinvolved.html
html www.worldofquotes.com/author/Dr.+Haim+Ginott/1/html
Holding Carter Jr:: https://www.guideposts.org/there-are-two-lasting-bequests-we.
Crudel: https://livelovelifealways.wordpress.com/.../kids-spell love-t-i-m-e-john-
Gibran: allpoetry.com/Children-Chapter-IV *The Prophet*
Douglas: www.brainyquote.com/quotes/quotes/f/frederickd201574.html
Mead: http://www.brainyquote.com/quotes/quotes/m/margare me133350.html
Carson: http://www.childrennatureandyou.org/quotes.html
Fred Rogers: http://www.fredrogers.org/parents/#sthash.WhrRhkvq.dpuf
https://giftedandtalented.com/spotlight/-/blogs/kids-and-smiles
http://www.romancatholic.kingston.on.ca/WEB%20SITE%20-%20ATTACHMENTS/marriage_2.pdf
http://entertainmentguide.local.com/family-team-building-game-ideas-10376.html
www.highlights.com/
http://theartofsimple.net/_the-importance-of-family-rituals/
http://www.forbes.com/sites/_reneesylvestrewilliams/2011/11/23/raising-children-the-role-of aunts-and-uncles/
http://www.rodneyohebsion.com/lakota.htm
http://www.cbn.com/family/parenting/goodwyn_MakeMemori es.aspx

www.artists helpingchildren.org wayschildrencanvolunteer.html and birthday.com/ideas/the-gift-of-giving-to-others-in-decem- ber.
ww.artistshelpingchildren.org/wayschildrencanvolunteer.html
http://fox4kc.com/2015/08/31/birthday-girl-asks-for-teddy-bears-for-kids-in-need-in-place-of-gifts/
http://www.atyourlibrary.org/passiton/preserve-memories-create-family-time-capsule
https://www.bobdylan.com/us/songs/forever-young and Copyright © 1973 by Ram's Horn Music; renewed 2001 by Ram's Horn Music
Songwriters: Sillers, Tia Sanders, Mark I Hope You Dance lyrics © Sony/ATV Music Publishing LLC, Universal Music Publishing Group
http://www.lyricsfreak.com/l/lee+ann+womack/i+hope+you+dance_20082214.html
http://www.annuinstitute.org/index_files/Page1002.htm\
http://scoutingmagazine.org/_issues/0009/a-rite.html#sbarc
http://www.seminolenation.org/camping.shtml
http://www.ymcaofpittsburgh.org/indian-guide-princess-program/
Greatest Love of All was written by Michael Masser & the late Linda Creed. Sung by Whitney Houston
http://genius.com/Whitney-houston-greatest-love-of-all-lyrics
www.outwardbound.org/
https://www.facinghistory.org/
motl.org/
http://blog.lovewell.org/
http://ideas.hallmark.com/quinceanera-ideas/what-is-a-quinceanera/
http://www.waldorfatlant.org/academics_lower_g5.php
http://www.thegrahamschool.org/contact
http://www.kindspring.org/story/ view.php ?sid = 7854
http://www.dolphincommunicationproject.org/index.php/shop

adopt-a-dolphin
http://www.pbs.org/parents/special/article-5-ways-kids-can-serve-communities.html
www.audensociety.org/vivianfoster.html
http://womenshistory.about.com/od/quotes/a/marian_edelman.htm
https://www.yahoo.com/ parenting/9-ways-to-teach-your-kids-about-love-without-120810690328.html
https://www.yahoo.com/ parenting/5-year-olds-touching-act-of-kindness-toward-119373307062.html
http://www. washingtonpost.com/lifestyle/kidspost/busy-kids-take-time-to-help-others/2014/01/02/79e7e9b6-70bc-11e3-8b3f-b1666705ca3b_story.html
http://www.chcatlanta.org/about
tolerance.org/youth-united
http://www. handsonatlanta.org/
www.brainyquote.com/quotes/quotes/a/audreyhepb126745.html

Chapter 4

PARENTING

Parent Talks (Seminars)

I have been asked to talk at Mom's Groups, Family Retreats, Libraries, PTAs, and Curriculum Nights on different themes. Below I will be sharing some of my thoughts that I talk about.

Feedback

"It was wonderful to have you speak to our parents." (Parent Facilitator at a school)

Talk on Parenting

To Mom's Groups, Family Retreats, and Libraries, (one hour)
I may just talk to the parents, and/or share a short **Story Time** for the children.

A Sample of an Agenda for a Talk on Parenting

o Introduce myself/my background: Julienne Marks retired. Children's Librarian at a Regional Library, teacher, museum educator, peace educator, chairperson of *Parenting Communication Workshop, How To Talk So Kids Will Listen*™ and *Siblings Without Rivalry*™ both by Adele Faber and Elaine Mazlish for many years, now volunteering working with children and parents. (Head Start, *Waldorf School* and sharing *Parenting Communication Workshops.)*
o Importance of reading to children even after they learn to read. Have fun with it.
o Some examples of experiences to do with children:

74

- Adventure walks
- Spend time in Nature
- Listening to music
- Moving at home (dance)
- Look at beautiful art
- Talk and listen about things that are important to your child
- Share your interests with your child
- Have fun
- Spend time with your child not only to discipline or help with academics but to have fun.
- Play (let your little child out) with your child. Allow your child to have free play
- Here are some *Mrs. Marks' Sparks* which are from books and my experiences/pebbles. Please look in this **Chapter** for an explanation and more **Sparks**
- Under a child's behavior is their emotion. Find out what it is and be your child's "emotion coach" (Kurcinka's book *Kids, Parents, and Power Struggles*)
- Your child is unique/special, the only one in the world, as is everyone else
- Watch your expectations
- Don't compare with siblings, cousins, and other children
- You have rights, you count
- Mutual respect
- The key is to *communicate* now so for the teen years you have a baseline (basis) for *communicating*
- Child will physically go away and then look back at you (2's and teens)
- Do not end your conversation with your child with okay? You are then asking your child to give their opinion. (Thanks, Bill)
- You are your child's model

- *Family Nights.* Please see **Chapter 3** for more information.
- Begin with one's strengths.
- There are usually alternative choices in solving life's problems.
- I believe that forgiveness is quite important for both children and parents.
- I believe that being grateful for what we have (for both children and parents) is very important.
- I don't believe children are "out to get you" or are manipulating you. There is a need or emotion not being fulfilled.
- Use humor that is not damaging to anyone.
- If you have more than one child, have alone time with each one daily.
- Have Dinner together talking and listening: What made you laugh today, what positive thing happened to you, negative?
- Hugs and saying I love you often.
- Note your child's interest/passion/hobbies/collections.
- Encourage this. On refrigerator keep list of questions, then go to the library and get some books to answer them.
- Think about what values you want to instill in your child. (By modeling, actions, books, etc.)
- What type of home environment do you want?
- Encourage imagination/creativity/curiosity.
- My view of screen time: (TV, computer, computer games, DVDs, iPads, etc.) It is the act of watching that is negative. Please see *The Plug in Drug* by Marie Winn and the American Academy of Pediatrics. Please see in this **Chapter** under Talk under Technology for more information.

Following are some thoughts/ideas/concepts from *Parenting Communication Workshops* I share: *How To Talk So Kids Will Listen™* and *Siblings Without Rivalry™* by Adele Faber and Elaine Mazlish

- Acknowledge, acknowledge, acknowledge
- Brainstorm/**problem solve**
- Siblings are separate and unequal
- Engaging children's cooperation
- Punishments verses logical consequences
- How to encourage autonomy
- Freeing children from playing roles
- Mediate
- Active listening

I share with the parents about the following Workshops:
The two workshops, *How to Talk So Kids Will Listen™* and *Siblings Without Rivalry™* are based on the work of the late child psychologist Dr. Haim Ginott. (*Between Parent and Child*) These workshops were developed by Adele Faber and Elaine Mazlish, award winning authors, (*How to Talk So Kids Will Listen and Listen So Kids Will Talk, Siblings Without Rivalry, Liberated Parents, Liberated Children: Your Guide to a Happier Family*) lecturers, who studied with Dr. Ginott. Faber and Mazlish developed these workshop kits whose goals are for parents to communicate more effectively with their children by experiencing and learning skills and techniques in a fun way. We will be listening to their voices via CDs. There are also role plays and discussions. There is a **Reminder Card** which summarizes what we learn each week and homework to try with your children what we learned and then come back to the next session to share.

The first Workshop, *How To Talk So Kids will Listen™* is seven weeks one and one-half hours.

Julienne Marks

The second Workshop, *Siblings Without Rivalry*™ is six weeks one and one-half hours. Please check our **Chapter 2** under Retirement for information about these workshops.

I also share that at my home once a month my husband and I host a Parenting Support Group to support and continue the *connections* made at the Workshops.

Feedback

"Based on Dr. Ginott's philosophy you suggested to the audience to acknowledge the feelings of an individual whether it be a child or an adult. You gave real life examples and also explained that no individual is the same." (contact person)

"The children ranging in age from infants to three years thoroughly enjoyed interacting with you during the **Story Time** you gave. They especially loved your choice of books involving animals noses and sounds. The mothers in attendance benefited greatly from your parenting tips and words of encouragement. How wonderful that two mothers in attendance registered for your parenting workshop beginning shortly." (The President of a Mom's group) (Thanks, Sarah)

A Talk About Cooperation VS Competition, Conflict Resolution, Television, War Toys, and Peace

"Condensing the myths of cooperation vs competition, basics of conflict resolution, television violence, the impact of war toys, and fostering peace in children by emphasizing positive differences made the one-hour presentation a stimulating and rapidly paced evening. Your positive approach to fostering peace in our children and our world is well inspirational. Noting the interest of questions about conflict resolution, would you consider speaking in greater detail to us about conflict resolution at a later Parent Education meeting?" (President of a Preschool) (Thanks, Geri)

Please see My Book, *Multiculturalism And Peace*, for more information on these topics.

Indoor Activities for Children

This talk was about suggestions to do when the weather is not good or one wants the children to be indoors or the child wants to be inside. There was a survey that the parent and child could do together with questions such as:
o Would the child rather play alone or with someone?
o Does the child like to play inside or outside?
o Does the child like to do things with their hands or read a book or both?
o Does the child enjoy talking to other people?
o What is the child interested in?
From these questions and others, one could try and figure out the child's interests and what could be a possible hobby or hobbies. Samples of possible activities were shared such as reading, coloring, doing Science Experiments, pretending, making crafts, etc. There was a packet/booklet with questions that each parent received for their child/children with examples of things children could do including drawing, yoga, making maps, doing experiments, taking items apart, listening to music, looking at pictures, etc.

Feedback

"Your discussion together with your booklet has helped us become more aware that each child has different needs and interests. When we focus on this, we can help them become more of a creative person." (parent from a Mom's group)
"The sensitive, practical, and comprehensive program you shared with us was quite an enlightening experience. The proof was found in the lively discussions, provoked by your fascinating ideas, heard throughout the lunchroom immediately

following your talk." (Director and parent of a Mom's Group) (Thanks, Sharon)

Pleasurable Reading/Reading for the Fun of It

I wanted to give a talk about "Pleasurable Reading/ Reading for the Fun of It" or other names such as "The Joys of Reading" or "Enjoyable Reading for Pleasure." Besides reading for school work or for a job, there is Reading for Pleasure. It can also be called reading what we want, recreational reading, reading for enjoyment, free voluntary reading, independent reading, lifelong reading, self-selection of books, hooked on books, freedom to read, or having a love affair with reading. As I was preparing for this talk, I found many research articles. I put together a notebook of these articles on this topic. Please note article *Good News! They Are Reading!* by Cindy Long, *NEA Today (National Education Association) Winter 2016*

Don't you enjoy books you have chosen yourself? Please note, *Reading for Pleasure*: a Research Overview.

I gave this talk at a library. I sincerely believe that one way to get a child to be a lifelong reader is to listen to what they are interested in and recommend books based on this interest; for example, if the child is a preschooler who loves dinosaurs, get him/her books on dinosaurs. Nonfiction books are wonderful for this age (for example, *The Eyewitness/ Dorling Kindersley books*). I have seen very young children devour (not really) these books on animals, astronomy, and the body so enjoying the photographs and pictures. I believe this is the first step to reading.

As a Youth Services librarian I was saddened how many children were turned off to reading. I wanted to share what I have been observing with children and hearing from parents and teachers in the library and as a teacher, in regard to reading for pleasure in Georgia, Florida, and New York.

Many Pebbles to Make a Difference

A Sample of **PR (Public Relations)** for: "A Youth Services Librarian's Scoop on Children Reading for Pleasure." or "Pleasurable Reading" "Reading for the Fun of It."

Date:
Time: Usually an evening
Adults only
Join us for a talk concerning the importance of children reading for pleasure. There will be a question and answer period as well.

For this program, a staff member made an excellent collage sharing great pictures of people reading. I especially loved the one with a child reading under his covers with a flashlight. (Thanks, Becky)

Some ways to encourage "Pleasurable Reading"
"Reading for the Fun of It" **Agenda**

+ Have your child see you reading. It lets your children know you regard reading as a valued activity in your home and that you relax with books, as well as, learn from them. Children model after you. Let them see you reading all types of materials.
+ Take a book wherever you go and encourage your child to also.
+ Make a regular (weekly) visit to the library to get books of interests and for pleasure reading.
+ Encourage children to pick out their own books. Encourage them to browse.
+ Find out what your child's interests are. Encourage that. Keep a list on the refrigerator of a child's questions and topics they seem interested in that you can take on your library's visits.
+ Continue to read aloud to children even when they are reading by themselves.

81

Julienne Marks

Feedback from "Pleasurable Reading" "Reading for the Fun of It"

"I was given a list of tips to help with my child's comprehension, as well as follow up books that could further my daughter's interest." (Thanks, Brandi)

The Importance of Libraries

Throughout my career as a librarian, I have given talks about the importance of libraries to both adults and children. Having worked in libraries for over 15 years, mostly in Youth Services (children), I know that libraries can offer children and parents books, *programs*, and *connections*. Librarians get to know what type of book a specific child might be interested in. I believe libraries are about *connection,* support, and listening. Fun, informative *programs* can touch patrons, even if only one patron shows up. In one of the "Creative Writing workshops" I gave, a child wrote for the first time about his feelings about his parents' divorce. He told me that he was grateful for having this opportunity at this workshop so he could write his feelings. Please see My Book, *Education in Different Environments,* under Libraries for information about this *program.*

I remember once reading, I think in the *American Libraries Association Magazine*, about the importance of *connections* with one patron vs statistics and how many patrons come into the library.

Talks on technology including **TV, DVDs**, computers, computer games, smart phones, iPads, tablets, Kindles, etc.
I have given several talks on this subject sharing with the adults about screen time. More and more studies and books are coming out stating that technology can have both positive and negative results for children.

82

As a parent and grandparent, I know how exhausting it is being and playing with children. One sometimes needs some space which I believe a parent needs and deserves to relax, cook, eat, play, do nothing, dream, etc. but using TV, DVDs or other electronic devices as a babysitter may not be such a good ideas as many articles and books are stating.

A parent needs some space. Parents may be giving their very young children iPads or their phone to play games to "quiet" them. Doesn't that say something? It "quiets" them. Now it seems everywhere you go, you see very young ones with iPads or on the parent's phone. Yes, they are being quiet, but what is happening to their brains? Other possibilities to "quiet" them include giving them paper, crayons, coloring books, including the Anti-coloring Book Series by Susan Striker, (Susan@SusanStriker.com), stickers, color forms, (vinyl adhesive toy set produced under the Colorforms brand.) etc. or if possible get a babysitter, perhaps another parent you trust, etc.

Children tune out so much more often nowadays. They are often shown DVDs, at camps, at afterschool programs, at school even in preschools! It seems children often do not play or interact with real people. At the library, children would often ask for books with the main characters from TV or DVDs. Often children's conversations and play acting are about DVD or TV characters or lessons learned from them. (For example, younger and younger children are learning about ghosts, zombies, vampires from DVDs and getting scared.) Board games also are being sold with TV characters. (Monopoly now has themes as Mickey Mouse, Star Wars and Sponge Bob.) It seems screens are everywhere, preschools, schools, many restaurants, airports, doctor offices, car repair places, and now even at the gas pump!

I found many parents did not realize that the American Academy of Pediatrics feels that screen time for children under two has no educational benefit and leaves less time for interacting with other people and playing. Exposure to technology: Ages three - five should be restricted to one hour per day and ages six – eight restricted to two hours per day. Parents and teachers please be aware of the following organizations or guides to help you share with your children.

Some TV/radio and commercials are so negative/derogatory about relationships and behavior. *Television and Children.*

The Center for Media Literacy works to connect the curriculum of the schools with the home.

Don't Buy It Guide for Teachers talks about how to realize the ideas behind making food look great on TV.

The goal of *Commercial Alert* is to prevent the commercial culture from using children to buy its products.

I would encourage my daughter while watching TV at home to say or yell out "Commercial!" when a commercial comes on; thus realizing that the commercial is trying to "sell" you something. Plus while using any technology to realize/see what people (advertisers) are trying to sell you with the popup ads. This is an idea for parents to remind their children to do this.

There are many commercials that show a smiling (usually) woman cleaning the house. Few people enjoy cleaning the house. Share from *Free to Be You and Me by* Marlo Thoms, *Housework* by Carol Channing.

Books to check out:
Failure to Connect: How Computers Affect Our Children's Minds—for Better and Worse by Jane Healy
The Plug-in Drug by Marie Winn
Parenting: Unplug Your Kids From the Digital World! 18 Rules on how to Teach Your Child to Reconnect with the Real World in a Digital Age by Yao.

I can't tell you how often parents would come into the library with their very young children and ask me what DVDs I would recommend for their child or ask their young child to pick some out. I wanted to say to them to get a book instead!

I remember a Mom told me at the library that one of the games on a children's program on the computer scared her child and the child was having nightmares. Children see differently than adults and different things can scare them.

It is quite interesting what happened to *Baby Einstein* videos for false advertising, saying that by watching them, your baby will become gifted. The Company had to actually return money to purchasers.

Now it seems children and parents at dinner are texting or checking their phones.

I saw on a TV commercial two teens using their smart phones during dinner with their parents. The parents exchange a questionable look. In the next scene the father is typing on a typewriter. The teens look at their Dad and put down their smart phones. He made his point. Wonderful.

Even during lunch at school children are not talking face to face but using their phones. Please check out Sherry Turkle's article, *Making the Case for Face to Face In An Era of Digital Conversation* 9/26/15. Ms. Turkle also has written the following books you may want to check out: *Life on the Screen: Identity in the Age of the Internet, The Second Self: Computers and the Human Spirit, and Alone Together: Why We Expect More from Technology and Less from Each Other.*

I have heard of parents saying during certain times, (mealtime) there will be no screens and grandparents saying when you come for a visit, it is you I want to see and listen to. No screens. I so honor that!

The line between the real world of interaction and the technology world no longer seems to exist to middle schoolers. *CNN's Anderson Cooper's 360 Degree Breaks News About Teens and Social Media Provocative Two–Year Investigation.*

Julienne Marks

"Sometimes our light goes out, but is blown again into instant flame by an encounter with another human being." by Albert Schweitzer.

Another book of interest is *Screen Time: How Electronic Media- From Baby Videos to Educational Software- Affects Your Young Child* by Lisa Guernsey.

There is an interesting official week (of course it can be anytime and for any amount of time, a day, a few days, a week, or an entire year) called **Screen Free Week**. In *Atlanta Parent* May 2015, please check out *From Screen-Focused to Screen Savvy* pages 18-21. Just turn off all technology in your home.

Screen Free Week could be sponsored by a school, library, etc. offering alternative suggestions as well as encouraging the student's creativity. **Screen Free Time Week** would be a time of creating, exploring, reading, daydreaming, playing, etc. by unplugging technology. Many libraries now give out idea sheets during this week. A *Waldorf School* shared ideas of screen-free activities for at home (for example, fix something, learn about native trees and flowers in your area) plus activities at the school after school hours for parents and children such as classic games day, singing, free range woods day, play with a box day. I had a patron who did the **Screen Free Week** both at home and in her classroom and introduced it at her school. She was so amazed how much more her own children played well together and were so creative and that in her classroom the class seemed calmer and also more creative. (Thanks, Anne)

Screen time takes away from family time and being "really" together, as well as daydreaming, being alone with oneself, and thinking. Please check out these books, *Unplugged: Ella Gets Her Family Back* by Pedersen and *Blackout* by Rocco.

Some examples of other articles on this topic:
Kaiser Foundation 2010, Active Healthy Kids Canada 2012
Common Sense Media 2013

Many Pebbles to Make a Difference

Cris Rowan, who is a pediatric occupational therapist, is asking parents, teachers and the government to ban the use of all handheld devices for children under 12 years old. In the article are ten research evidenced reasons for this ban.

Ten reasons why handheld devices should be banned for children under the age of 12 by Rowan

Call Me Mean (Maybe): Why I Won't Get a Smartphone for My Teen, by Lisa Rinkus

Children Are Competing With Devices For Uninterrupted Time With Their Parents by Alessia Santoro, 7/14/15

8 Ways Screens are Ruining Your Family Life mentions the following book: *The Big Disconnect: Protecting Childhood and Family Relationships in the Digital Age* by Catherine Steiner-Adair Center for Media Literacy

A Story

The Stranger

A few months before I was born, my Dad met a stranger who was new to our small town. From the beginning, Dad was fascinated with this enchanting newcomer, and soon invited him to live with our family. The stranger was quickly accepted and was around from then on.

As I grew up I never questioned his place in our family. In my young mind, each member had a special niche. My parents were complementary instructors. Mum taught me good from evil and Dad taught me to obey. But the stranger was our storyteller. He would keep us spellbound for hours on end with adventures, mysteries and comedies. He could hold our whole family spellbound for hours each evening.

If I wanted to know about politics, history, or science, he always knew the answers about the past, understood the present, and even seemed to predict the future! He took my family to our first major league baseball game. He made me laugh and he made me cry. The stranger never stopped talking, but Dad never seemed to mind. Sometimes Mum would get up quietly while the rest of us were shushing each other to listen to what he had to say and she would go to the kitchen for peace and quiet. (I wonder now if she every prayed for the stranger to leave.)

Dad ruled our household with certain moral convictions. But this stranger never felt obligated to honor them. Profanity, for example, was not allowed in our house, not from us, our friends, or any visitors. Our longtime visitor, however, got away with four-letter words that burned my ears and made Dad squirm and my mother blush. My Dad didn't permit the liberal use of alcohol but the stranger encouraged us to try it on a regular basis. He made cigarettes look cool, cigars manly, and pipes distinguished. He talked freely (much too freely!) about sex. His comments were sometimes blatant, sometimes suggestive, and generally embarrassing.

I now know that my early concepts about relationships were influenced strongly by the stranger. Time after time, he opposed the values of my parents, yet he was seldom rebuked... And NEVER asked to leave. More than fifty years have passed since the stranger moved in with our family. He has blended right in and is not nearly as fascinating as he was at first. Still if you could walk into my parents' den today, you would still find him sitting over in his corner, waiting for someone to listen to him talk and watch him draw his pictures.

His name?...

We just call him 'TV.'

He has a wife now... we call her 'Computer.'

Their first child is 'Cell phone.'

Many Pebbles to Make a Difference

Second child is 'iPad.'

Author Unknown.

Having Fun with Children/Play

I believe parenting is not only about a child's education and the sharing of values. Parents need to be reminded to have fun with your children. And fun may be different for different people. Play is one way of having fun with your child.

Play together, board games, pretend, etc. Some helpful books on this topic include *The Power of Play: Learning what Comes Naturally* by David Elkind, (See **Chapter 7** for more information on this book.) *Playful Parenting* by Lawrence Cohen, *A Child's Work: The Importance of Fantasy Play* by Vivien Pauley, and *The Importance of Play in Promoting Healthy Child Development and Maintaining Strong Parent-Child Bonds* by Kenneth R. Ginsburg, MD, MSEd and the Committee on Communications and the Committee on Psychosocial Aspects of Child and Family Health.

Play something you enjoy. Let your "little child" out What did you like to do as child? *Wishcraft* by Sher talks about this. Share your interests with each other. For example, I enjoy reading, acting out books, singing, coloring, and being in nature. As a Mom and grandmother, I shared many of these things with my daughter and grandson, as a teacher to my students and parents, and as a Youth Services Librarian to my patrons in my *programs.*

Please check out this article about using play to make transitions with your children. *Let's Take a Bath in the Magical Forest by Dawson, Moving Through the Day with Play, Mothering*, September.October, 2000.

Play Outside/Look at/Observe Nature. Drink in Nature. Some books on this topic include*: Last Child in the Woods: Saving Our Children from Nature – Deficit Disorder* by Richard Louv and *Sharing Nature With Your Children* by Joseph Cornell. For more information on the former book see **Chapter 7.**

What does your child like to do for fun? As a child, my daughter liked to act and plan shows. Now she is a drama teacher at a high school. What do you like to do for fun? I love to have a belly laugh, blow bubbles, look at the clouds, listen to music, have deep talks with good friends, and share what I have seen. My daughter told me that one of her fondest memories of us doing things together was looking at clouds, waiting for my husband to come home from work. My grandson enjoys sports, chess, acting, singing, science, taking things apart, history, and reading.

When children develop an interest, hobby, collection, sport, the arts, etc., it may give them meaning in their life and perhaps help to keep them out of the negative aspects of life. Instead of watching TV or DVDs, using a computer, or being on your cell phone, or iPads, BE TOGETHER. Share life experiences by talking and listening, reading the classics to your children (even if the child is reading on their own), and doing an art project, go for a nature walk, listen to classical music, go to a museum, see a play, play with them, playing cooperative board games, etc. Please see My Book, *Multiculturalism And Peace,* for more information about Cooperative games.

Please also see and share with your child *Time to Play,* July/August 2015 *Cobblestone* for some interesting articles on play including: *Play in the City, America's Pastime, Being a Good Sport*, etc.

WHAT ARE *Mrs. Marks' Sparks?*

Mrs. Marks' Sparks are ideas I have picked up along the way by experience, my reading, and conversations with others that I feel are important to share in my presentations. They are not necessarily original to me. *Mrs. Marks' Sparks* may be ideas, thoughts, beliefs, opinions, values for us to think about. I hope some resonate with you. Do any call/speak out to you? If so, try a *Spark* and then another and then another. It may be relevant information that I want to pass on. Sometimes at the end of some of my *programs* I might share a *Mrs. Marks' Spark* that was appropriate. It is like throwing a pebble or ripple to others and perhaps seeing how many people respond shaking their head in agreement.

Feedback

Mrs. Marks' Sparks were like "little nuggets of wisdom and love." (Thanks, Julia)

"I loved your little words of wisdom and encouragement for all of us Moms." (a patron) (Thanks, Betsy)

⊥ *Mrs. Marks' General Sparks*

- o Everybody has a life story to share. This is my work story. What is yours?
- o Change takes time and perseverance. Be patient with yourself. "If nothing ever changed, there'd be no butterflies." Author Unknown Just when the caterpillar thought the world was over, she became a butterfly.
- o "If you think you're too small to make a difference, spend a night with a mosquito." African proverb
- o Some ways of speaking: Saying:
  - I suggest
  - Please consider
  - Does that make sense? (Thanks, Anne and Valerie)
  - Let me suggest this
  - How can I help?

I noticed that….

- During my programs, I would give a choice to children and parents saying, "If you would like." For example, "If you would like, cover your eyes or stand up."
- One never really can get something free. Examine what one needs to do to get the free "thing."
- Walk your talk. Listen to yourself. Be kind to yourself and others.
- "We teach what we need to learn." I firmly believe in this statement.
- "We teach best what we most need to learn." by Bach
- Express one's feelings and listen to others express theirs.
- I believe we need to do for others, help each other: a mission, service, or be a steward.
- It is important in realizing that people may communicate in different ways.
- When a door closes, a window opens.
- Then, when it seems we will never smile again, life comes back.
- *Feel the Fear and Do it Anyway* by Dr. Susan Jeffers. I wrote her and she called me. WOW!
- Everyone has good in them.
- We can learn from everyone: seniors, younger and older children, adults, and animals.
- Learn to trust one's intuition (gut feeling).
- When one feels good about oneself, one doesn't need to "prove" anything to others.
- Set personal boundaries /priorities/goals
- Taking responsibility for what one does (your actions) and not blame out or scapegoat others is something we all need to work on. And then to deal with it.
- Everyone's Perception is their truth. We see things from our point of view, our experiences. Please look at

Six Blind Mice by Ed Young and *Things are Not Always Black or White* by Judie Paxton in *Chicken Soup of the Kid's Soul* by Jack Canfield on this topic. Please see My Book, *Multiculturalism And Peace,* for more information on Perception.

Mrs. Marks' Family and Parenting Sparks are some examples of philosophy, things to do, and examples of spending quality time with your family. Adapt these to your particular family. I have also added some books and websites with articles about a topic. Some are for you, others are for your children, and some are for you both. I have drawn on things that I believe are important but please note there is so much more out there about children.

o Parents set up how the family works, how kind and how helpful family members are to each other, how everyone treats each other, and what is acceptable and unacceptable to the family.
o Think about what type of home environment you want. Think about what your goals are as parents. Talk with your children about life and our purpose and why we are here on earth.
o Think about what values/character you want to instill in your child. Your values can be shared using all types of books. Check out these books: *40 Ways to Teach Your Child Values* by Paul Lewis, *How to Generate Values in Young Children* by Sue Spayth Riley, *A Call to Character* Editors Colin Greer & Herbert Kohl, *The Moral of the Story, Folktales for Character Development* by Bobby and Sherry Norfolk, *The Spiritual Life of Children* by Robert Coles, *Being Your Best* and *Character Building for Kids 7-10* both by Barbara A. Lewis, *Character Education: Book Guide for Teachers, Librarians, and Parents* by McElmeel, *Books that Build Character: A Guide to Teaching Your*

Child Moral Values Through Stories by Kilpatrick, Wolfe, Wolfe. *What Do You Stand For? For Kids, A Guide for Building Character* (for children) by Lewis.
Your Letters, Mothering, November/ December 2000, by Corina Schad, says something interesting about this subject.

- Every family has their own rules, norms, and values. For example, not to hurt others, be kind to oneself and others, work together to do chores around the house, etc.
    - See *Value Tales* by Johnson for a collection of life stories/biographies based on values we can all believe in plus an imaginary child orientated conscience. These books were used by my daughter, my brother's children, and now my grandson. All of the children so enjoyed them.
    - A *ValueTales Treasury: Stories for Growing Good People* by Spencer Johnson and illustrated by Dan Andreasen for Grades 2-14
    - Based on the original stories, these new *ValueTales®* have been reimagined and reillustrated to appeal to a new generation of children.
    - I have a few of these last ones and they also are wonderful. Helping children to listen to their true voice is important.
- An inspriring way to share good valves and seeing positive role models. I see posters on billboards, etc. Please check out *Foundation for a Better Life*. Pass It On! Free posters (for example "Eats flies, Dates a Pig, Hollywood Star- Live Your Dreams and a photo of Kermit" and "Photo of Mona Lisa with the words Smile Pass it On") for schools and nonprofits. One can also watch moving commercials such as "Memories Remember When."

- Discussions at *Family Nights* and *Family Meetings* about values is another possibility. Please see **Chapter 3** for more information.
- What is your philosophy of life? (your truths) Share with your children.
- What does your child think? My daughter and grandson would ask me: Why are we here?
- What are your priorities?
- The Golden Rule has similar meanings in many religions: "Do unto others as you would have them do unto you." Someone once said to me since we are all different what you may like, I may not. For example, say I love receiving cards for my birthday. And someone else couldn't care about birthday cards. So by my following the Golden Rule I would give a card, perhaps to someone who really doesn't want one.
  - Then there is The Silver Rule "Do not do unto others as you would not have them do unto you."
  - Do not do to others that which would anger you if others did it to you. Socrates (Greek Philosopher, circa 470-399 BC)
  - *The Golden Rule* by Cooper is an interesting book on this topic.
  - Note the poster of the Golden Rule of different religions

I want to Commend:
- 'Zaxby's Kidz Care'
- The Chick-fil-A Kids Club - As gifts children receive books on values, (some of the books are *Value Tales*) nonfiction, abridged classic stories. I also commend Chick-fil-A for closing on Sundays as this is part of their beliefs. They walk their talk.
- Something else wonderful at Chick-fil-A for parents. Order at the drive through and then walk into the restaurant and your table is set with your food. WOW!

And For Adults:
- ▪ Chipotle aims to cultivate thought on its packaging.

See lists of book on specific character traits:
Honesty/Lying/Truth: *Lying Up a Storm* by Cook
Lying (Help Me Be Good Books About series) by Berry
Howard B. Wigglebottom and the Monkey on His Back: A Tale About Telling the Truth by Binkow
The Berenstain Bears and the Truth by Berenstain
The Empty Pot by Demi
The Value of Honesty: A Story about Confucius (Value Tales) by Johnson
Jamaica and the Substitute Teacher by Havill (cheating on a test)
The Emperor's New Clothes by Andersen
The Honest –to- Goodness Truth by McKissack
A Pair of Red Clogs by Matsuno
The Boy Who Cried Wolf by Sommer
A Penny's Worth of Character by Stuart
Caring/Charity/Helping Others/Unselfishness:
When I Care about Others by Spellman (*The Way I Feel series*)
Flicka, Ricka, Dicka and the Strawberries by Lindman
Helping Others by Raum (*Kids Making a Difference series*)
The Snow Walker by Wetterer (*On My Own History*)
The Empty Pinata by Ada (unselfishness)
Patience:
Subira, Subira by Mollel
Magic Seeds of Patience by Haddi
Children's Virtues: P is for Patience by Jones
Slowly, Slowly, Slowly, said the Sloth by Eric Carle
Let's Talk About Patience by Berry
The Carrot Seed by Krauss

Being Responsible for What One Does/Accountability
It's Not My Fault by Cook (*Responsible Me series*)
It's Not My Fault! by Carlson
It's Not My Fault! by Mason
The Summer My Father Was Ten by Brisson (also mistakes)
Kindness/Random Acts of Kindness/Compassion:
The Kindness Quilt by Wallace
Small Acts of *Kindness* by Vollbracht
Kindness: Treasury of Buddhist Wisdom for Children and Parents by Conover
Heartprints by Hallinan
Kindness to Share From A-Z by Snow
Invisible Boy by *Ludwig*
The Seven Gods of Luck by Kudler
Giving/Generosity:
Under the Lemon Moon by Fine (Mexico, generosity)
 (Thanks, Catalina)
Giving by Hughes
The Giving Box by Fred Rogers
The Giving Tree by Silverstein
Lend a Hand: Poems about Giving by Frank
The Book of Giving
Poems of Thanks, Praise and Celebration by Chorao
Reach Out and Give by Meiners *(Learning to Get Along series)*
The Perfect Orange: A Tale from Ethiopia by Araujo
(Toucan Tales Series Vol. 2) (selflessness)
The Littlest Angel by Tazewell, (the best gift is one that is hard to give)
An Orange for Frankie and *Gifts of the Heart* by Polacco
The Gift of the Magi by O'Henry (Lynch)
Kiki's Hats by Hanson (I know two women, who did this) (Thanks Sally and Vicki)
The Bremen Town Musicians and *The Elves and the Shoemaker* (*Grimm's Fairy Tales*)

Sharing How Kindness Grows by Shaw

Courage/Bravery:
Against the Odds, Four True Life Stories about Courage (Winner's Circle Values In Action ™series)
Spaghetti in a Hot Dog Bun by Dismondy
Courage by Waber, *Have Courage: A Book About Being Brave* by Meiners (*Being the Best Me series*)
The Brave Little Tailor (*Grimm's Fairy Tales*)
The Hole in the Dike by Green, illustrated by Carle
The Lighthouse Keeper's Daughter by Olson
Nessa's Fish by Luenn
Bright Star by Crew
Wringer by Spinelli
Thunder Cake by Polacco
Gratitude/Appreciation:
Gratitude Soup by Rosewood
Gratitude Journal for Kids: My Gratitude Journal by Mirabell Publishing.
Thankful:
The Thankful Book by Parr
Let's Be Thankful, I'm Thankful For So Many Things, and *I'm Thankful Each Day* by Hallinan,
Peanuts
Be Thankful by Schulz (also *Be: active, joyful, awesome, brave, kind, unique, loving, friends series*)
All of Me?: A Book of Thanks by Bang
The Secret of Saying Thanks by Wood.
- Another resource: Josephson Institute Center for Youth Ethics.
- *Learning to Be Good* by Turiel
- *Why Danish Parents (and the Kids) are Happier than Americans.*
- Have alone Family Time just with your family. But sometimes, due to the age and interests of your children, it might

be better not to do "together" family things all the time. Family Time may not be beneficial to the family. It might be better not to force this issue.

- Many parents idealize a picture of family celebrations and events and ignore possible negative undercurrents. It is important to choose which Family Times parents will push their children to attend. For example, insisting a teenager attend their elementary age sibling's sport event. Yes, it is important in a family to support each other but if the teenager is really not interested, it may be worse having her /him there. This may be a family value.

- A School Psychologist I worked with while I was teaching, told me that if I can suggest anything to my students' parents, ask them to do this: spend undivided alone time with each child at least five minutes each day with direct attention. Some parents I have talked to had dates with their children separately (sometime with one parent, sometime with both parents). Having this to look forward to may help when all your children want you at the same time. Also for only children, time with each parent is important. (Thanks, Sherry)

- I have heard very positive results from parents using this practice. I have suggested this each time I give the *Parenting Communication Workshops, How to Talk So Kids Will Listen*™ and *Siblings Without Rivalry*™ both by Adele Faber and Elaine Mazlish. For example, one stepmother went with her stepchild to pick out a kitten, while another parent uses 20 minutes every few days instead of daily. (Thanks, Deyvani)

- Please check out Chick-fil-A's: Daddy, Daughter-Mother, Son Date Nights and Chili's Daddy Daughter-Mother Son Night Out when they skyped.

- Knowing there will be times for them with their parent, may help a child when his parent is unavailable to them.

- Different children may need different forms of gestures of attention and acknowledgement. Please check out *The Five Love Challenges of Children* by Gary Chapman.
o Look at your child and who he is, and not what is wrong with them.
o Spend time with one's extended family or friends with really "being" with them.
o Be with your child, not only doing homework with them. (Whose homework is it?)
o I strongly believe that what we want to share with our children is that learning is fun, interesting, and enhances us as people, thus promoting lifelong learning.
o Share different experiences with your children: attend plays and concerts, go to different types of museums, look at beautiful art, (of The Great Masters), including photography, expose/listen to different types of music, including the different instruments, dance, drama, theatre games, skits, improvise, Readers' Theatre, plays on serious subjects, use puppets of different types, go to parks, hike, take walks, observe nature, play board games, play or watch sports, go bike riding, attend multicultural events, and of course traveling to see our world as a family. For example travel to see places made by man and places made by nature, and meet people who live differently than we do, etc.
  - Books on Learning about Art and Children: *Come Look With Me Series: World of Art, Landscape Art, Animals, Early American Art, Artists at Work, Women's Art, Asian Art, African American Art, Latin American Art, American Indian Art, Modern Art* by Blizzard, and *A Child's Book of Art: Great Picture, First Words* by Micklethwait, *13 Artists Children Should Know and 13 Paintings Children Should Know* by Wenzel. Also one can look up specific artists.
o Play classical music for you and your children to listen and move to. Three wonderful pieces are *The William Tell*

Overture by Rossini, *In the Hall of the Mountain King* by Edvard Grieg and John Philip Sousa's *Marches*.

o Share with your children who you are through your passions, interests, loves, collections, hobbies. Having a passion (something that excites you) /interest/hobby, plus helping others, makes us whole. Reaching out to others continues our humanity.

o *Helping Your Children Find their Passions* by Jessen. Each member of a family can embrace what they are interested in. If quitting needs to happen, let it happen.

o There is also a song/passion/quest within each child. You, the parent can help it come out.

o Be involved in an Intergenerational atmosphere. I was talking to a young Mom who is a musician. Near to July 4 she took her young children to an assisted living facility and they all sang patriotic songs, played the piano and violin. (Thanks, Jamie)

o If interested, have your child go to religious school, attend one's own religious services and/or other religions' services too. Share your traditions with others.

  ▪ I was asked to talk about Chanukah and Passover at my daughter's *Waldorf Schools*.

  ▪ We sent our daughter to a synagogue (Hebrew School) and to a Yiddish School.

o Make a point of meeting people of different religions, cultures, challenges, etc. and *communicating* with them by respecting others' traditions. Go to different cultures, Festivals/Fairs. All the following were great learning experiences for me. There are so many similar yet different aspects to religions.

  ▪ My daughter would visit a friend's home and help decorate her Christmas tree and sometimes attended Christmas Eve Services.

Julienne Marks

- One year when my husband and I were in Spain, we found a small church with guitars playing on Christmas Eve. It was amazing.
- I attended several Christian services with friends.
- I gave my *Parenting Communication Workshop, How To Talk So Kids Will Listen™* by Faber and Mazlish at a Hindu Temple. I found it so interesting that there were many similarities to a Jewish service. For example, the use of a Shofar and Conch. Then there is the Native American ceremony of smudging and incense.
- I went to a Buddhist Temple with a friend for a meditation service. (Thanks Kathleen)
- Being at the Western Wall in Israel was quite a moving experience for me.

o While on a trip with a group, someone shared with me his view of taking pictures. He felt that if you are busy taking photographs, those photos will be the only memories for you to share. But if you are in the "Moment" observing, then that will be the memory.

- At an Advent Ceremony at a *Waldorf School* parents were asked not to take photos but to be in the moment 'seeing' their child go through the maze, How interesting. *See Live in the Moment Savor the Moments* by Krupicka, *Atlanta Parent,* May 2015 page 13.

o Make your days special and memorable with your children.
o Try and keep track of your siblings as you grow. My siblings and I, although living in different parts of the United States, try and get together, minus children and husbands at least once a year and travel to different places. Please check out the last chapter in *Siblings Without Rivalry* by Adele Faber and Elaine Mazlish.
o Even when your children are grown there are positive things parents and adult children can do together. Keep up the communication and listening to each other.

- I have a friend with four adult children who put around 30 questions in a basket.When her family had finished eating, the basket was passed around. Everyone took four questions and they went around the table answering one question at a time and continued the pattern until everyone had answered their four questions. It was fun and there was much laughter. Some of the questions were: what is your favorite board game? a place you want to vacation to, what makes you mad? what is the best smell in the world? what is your special talent? (Thanks, Mae)
  There are no mistakes, only opportunities by Tina Fey
  There are no mistakes in life, only lessons by Robin Sharma

o Share with your children to use the words: challenge /opportunity/discovery/present/gift/obstacle instead of mistake. Tell them about your mistakes. Some believe there are no mistakes, only lessons and those lessons are repeated until they are learned. Mistakes can be positive for you and your child's growth on the journey of life. Step back and look at them.

- Mistakes can help you discover something you never knew before. I read that a Native American said that whenever she makes a mistake in her quilt, she welcomes it because "Imperfection is what makes one beautiful."

- "I like the fact that in ancient Chinese art, the great painters always include a deliberate flaw in their work. A human creation is never perfect." *A Circle of Quiet* by Madeleine L'Engle page 31.

- Check out the book, *The Gifts of Imperfection: Let Go of Who You Think You're Supposed to Be and Embrace Who You Are* by Brene Brown.

- "When I was young I observed that nine out of every ten things I did were failures, so I did ten times more work." George Bernard Shaw

- "Success is sweet, Mistakes are good food." (Thanks, Anne)
- "A mistake can be a present. It can help you discover something you never knew before." *How To Talk So Kids Will Listen and Listen So Kids Will Talk* by Faber and Mazlish.
- Read what Thomas Edison's remarks were about mistakes.
- Children's Books about Mistakes:
  A Big Mistake by Rinder
  Regina's Big Mistake by Moss
  Oops I Made a Mistake by Hood
  Beautful Oops by Slatzberg
  The Girl Who Never Made Mistakes by Pett
o Remember that life is often not fair and although one can't change bad situations, one can change how one views and acts (reacts) towards the situation.
o Children/Parents have choices with what actions they choose to do. What will you do?
o Try to give children one direction at a time. Giving them your full attention with eye contact, no cell phones, etc. A sad incident I observed. A Mom and her young child were at a bus stop. The child was trying to get his Mom's attention but the Mom was on the phone and continued to talk on the phone. Before cell phones, it used to be whenever the parent was on a land phone, the child seemed to need you. But now the parent seems to be on their cell or smart phone all the time.
  - What about in restaurants when there could be conversations? One notices more and more people are on their separate phone or tablets, entire families!!
  - A preschool teacher told me how sad it was to her to see parents dropping off their children to school being

on the phone and not even saying, "Goodbye, have a great day. I love you." (Thanks, Judy)

- I believe you don't always have to do your best. Can you imagine making every meal your best? Give yourself and your children some downtime. Many of us parents say, "Just do your best."
- Read together as a family either out loud or to oneself in the same room.
- Talk and listen to each other, but not as a drill time.
- *Helicopter Vs Free-Range. How About Common Sense Parenting?* by Johnston. I find this quite sad.
- *Free-Range Kids, How to Raise Safe, Self Reliant Children (Without Going Nuts With Worry)* by Skenazy. A patron recommended this book to me. The author made some interesting points. Check it out.
- *The Overprotected Kid* by Rosen *Atlantic,* April 14
- I just found this out: The term 'helicopter parent' was first used in Dr. Haim Ginott's 1969 book *Parents & Teenagers* by teens who said their parents would hover over them like a helicopter; the term became popular enough to become a dictionary entry in 2011. *What is Helicopter Parenting?* by Grablewski.
- Eat meals together. Perhaps say a prayer/blessing before and after the meal. Parents set the tone of the meals. Make them relaxed and comfortable. Talk and listen to each other. Talk about how the day went for all. Share what you are grateful for, something good that happened that day, something that may be upsetting you, and what made them laugh. In our family, we talk about our pits and peaks. (From Kardashians TV show as suggested by my daughter)
- My suggestion would be no devices at dinnertime.
- *Why Eating Family Meals Together is Still Important Today* by Lindsay Seaman, Eartheasy.com Posted Dec 8, 2011. The evening meal can be the only time the

family is together to talk and listen to each other, re-group, get support, learn family values, *connect* with each other, etc. But not as a drill time.

- Why should we eat dinner together more often? *The Family Dinner Project* by Fishel (also by Fishel, *Home for Dinner, Mixing Food, Fun and Conversation for a Happier Family and Healthier Kids.*)
- Stop and smell the roses and slow down. Some children's books that share this thought: *Grandfather and I* by Helen Buckley and *"Slowly, Slowly, Slowly," said the Sloth* by Eric Carle.

o Go on Adventure Walks: Take some plastic sandwich bags, staple them together with the opening facing out. As you walk, pick up acceptable things with your child like acorns, leaves, stones, etc. and put them into the plastic bags. When you get back home, you and your child can find information from books about what you've picked up or just keep it to refer back to.

o Have FUN!!!! Please see Having Fun with Children in this **Chapter** and Play.

o Work on having balance in the parent/child relationship.

o You are your child's refuge, safety, and advocate. Be aware of what is going on in the classroom and after school activities. Use your own common sense.

o I wanted our home to be a safe place for my daughter to be herself and to try on other identities. As Dr. Ginott suggests to parents, "Pick your battles."

o Finding and then being authentically/genuinely yourself is a lifelong journey. I believe when you are doing something and it resonates with you, you are being authentically you, that is what life is really about. *Simple Abundance* by Sarah Breathnach shares specific examples of being authentically yourself.

o When children see you being "yourself authentically," it gives them permission to do so also. Encourage your child to be authentically themselves.

> "This above all:
> To thine own self be true,
> And it must follow, as the night the day,
> Thou canst not then be false to any man."
> *Hamlet,* by William Shakespeare.

- Share who you are with your children.
- Your feelings count. When you need space or are not feeling well, tell your children. From this, they will learn it is okay to share their feelings with others.
- When you are angry tell your child you are angry using I statements but do not destroy the character of the child. This shows them it is okay to be angry. It is what you do with the anger that is important. Talk about what is acceptable to do when one is angry. For example, rip up paper, exercise, draw pictures of how you feel, punch a punching bag, or clay, etc.

o Children are watching us; we are their role models. Your values are shown by what you do. Build a home climate of your values. Values/convictions, lasting beliefs, and ideals shared by parents of what is good or bad and desirable or undesirable are shown by what a family does.

- Watch how young children play house. It may be what you sound like.

o I recommend reading the poem *Today* by Henry Matthew Ward

- Manners: Model for your children and spouse how you would like them to talk in regard to manners and simple courtesy towards others. For example: "Please pass the fruit," "Thank you for the bread," "May I please be excused?" "Please take your plate to the sink," "Yes / No

Sir/Ma'am," "Bless you." etc. See this book for more ideas. *The Importance of Teaching Manners* by Pam Myers, August 17, 2011 Child Development Institute.
- Here are some book titles on manners for children: For example, Manners/ Courtesy/ Politeness: *Manners Time* by Verdick, *Emily's Everyday Manners* by Post, *Time to Say "Please!"* by Willems, *Do Unto Otters: A Book About Manners* by Keller

o There are some characteristics or personality traits that can be both positive and negative in our children and ourselves. For example, by being focused one may not see all the possibilities; by being on time, one may not be spontaneous; and if one is very detail oriented, one may lose what one is trying to accomplish. Try and look at these traits both positively and negatively.

o Focus on the behavior one wants to see.

o Chores: Think about this: Do you want your children to receive an allowance for helping out in the family or are you a team and everyone needs to help out because they are part of your family? Allowance then is separate than chores. *Chores and Allowance: Should Parents Pay Kids for Chores?"* by Pamela Laney. You decide.

o I feel it is important to experience having no money and/or having money but not spending it only on "things" (also saving and giving to others less fortunate than the child) even if there is money available. *"Teach your Kids to Give, Save, and Spend Wisely."*

o Children are curious and learning all the time naturally. I believe this should be encouraged! Listen to your children's questions and their conversations. Notice your child's interests/passions. Keep a running list on the refrigerator of these questions or your child's interests so that when you go on your weekly trip to the library, your children can not only pick out pleasure books, they can refer back to this list for topics. Find people who are experts on topics of interest

of your child and have them talk to your child. Interest can
be sports, the arts, etc.

- My daughter seemed to enjoy seeing theater, acting,
  singing and dancing in plays when she was quite
  young. Realizing this she took classes in this. Now she
  is a theater High School teacher. She also tried flute,
  piano and gymnastics which she decided she didn't
  want to continue.

o Be aware of media, the materialness of the world, and the
environment and how it is affecting your children and you.

o I don't believe children are out to "get/manipulate us."
There is something going on with them. Their needs may
not be getting met. One needs to search to figure it out.

- Under a child's behavior is his/her emotions. Find out
  what the emotion is. Be your child's "emotion coach."
  From *Parents, Kids, and Power Struggles* by Mary
  Kurcinka.

- Feelings are neither right nor wrong. They just are
  (Heard on a "Marriage Encounter Weekend"). Please
  see **Chapter 6** for more information.

- Value the feelings of others, as well as your own.

- Encouragement is the most important skill adults can
  learn in helping children.

- *Children: The Challenge: The Classic Work on Improving Parent-Child Relations-Intelligent, Humane, and
  Eminently Practical* by Rudolf Dreikurs. Check this
  book!

  ♣ "A misbehaving child is a discouraged child."
  Positive Discipline by Jane Nelson. Please see
  Chapter 7, for more information.

o "You are special, as is everyone else." My daughter didn't
like hearing the last part of this statement as a child, because she felt it cancelled out the specialness. But as an
adult she realized how important the last part of the statement was.

- "Always remember that you are absolutely unique. Just like everyone else." Margaret Mead.
- Your child is the only one (with his/her own fingerprint) like him/her in the whole world. He/She is unique/special, as is everyone else.
- Try to not compare your child with their siblings, cousins, and other children. Expectations can work against you.
- Read the poem by Elizabeth Anne Richards Schurg *I'm Special*
- "When children know uniqueness is respected, they are more likely to put theirs to use." Dorothy Corkille Briggs.

o I believe a parents' role is to give their children boundaries and to say no when necessary.

o To say to your child: "I am not afraid of your strong feelings nor should you be. I will help you to stop."

o "It is okay to be ambivalent and have two conflicting thoughts."

o I believe it is best not to end your conversation with your child with "Okay?" That is giving a child the power to say "No" or negotiate with you. (Thanks, Bill)

o Sometimes we do not realize what T-shirts our children are wearing and what they are saying. May that have anything to do with how they are acting? For example, "Spoiled rotten!" "Mom will Do Whatever I Say."

o What words are in the songs your children are singing? Listen to the words of *Little Rabbit, Foo Foo,* and what it says about boppin over the head.

o "What you resist, persists" by Carl Jung (Thanks, Dawn)

o While traveling or at home: Have games, coloring, colorforms, stickers, snacks, play oral games such as Geography, note the license plates of cars, etc. I used to wrap up my daughter's old toys and she would think they were new. (I later told her they were already hers). I have fond memories of singing, listening to music, talking and having quiet time during our travels both as a child, a mother, and grandmother.

o Cat's Cradle, the string game is so much fun to do with your family. Helpful Books on this topic include: *Pull the Other One!* by Taylor, *Cat's Cradle* and *String Games from Around the World* by Johnson, *Cat's Cradle, Owl's Eyes: A Book of String Games* by Gryski.

o Encourage/share traditional games as jump rope, marbles, jacks, leap frog, hide and seek, follow the leader, card games, (like goldfish) and board games as checkers, Chinese checkers, Parcheesi, chess, and mancala.

o Sing with your child. Sing-alongs are so much fun. Share Traditional Songs, (like *I've been Working on the Railroad*) Up Activities: *Farmer in the Dell*.

o If you lie, children may model after you.

＋ I found in *Between Parent and Child* by Dr. H. Ginott (pages 65-71) and in *How To Talk So Kids Will Listen* and *Listen So Kids Will Talk* by Faber and Mazlish some information about lying and on their website under "Ask Adele and Elaine" under lying. Please check out their website for more information. Why do children lie? It may be due to fears and/or wishes.

▪ I remember seeing a TV commercial many years ago. A parent was telling his child not to steal. But the parent was using a towel that said the name of a hotel. What a hypocrite that parent was being with his child.

• Little white lies and big lies: *What White Lies Teach Your Child* by *Child Magazine*

• Have your children hear your voice, speaking and singing (not so many toys' voices.)

o Use positive thinking. "Positive thinking is about seeing the positive situation in your life and in the world.

111

o   Hugs are so important to us all. Virginia Satir said, "It takes four hugs a day to survive, eight hugs a day to maintain, and 12 hugs a day to grow and thrive."

o   Do you think it is important to say, "I love you" to your children often or is it your actions that show your love for them or a combination of both? An interesting question to ponder.

o   I believe every child (and you also) is gifted, having both strengths and weaknesses. Build up your child's (and your) strengths.

o   Congratulate yourself for your strengths, creativity, and resourcefulness, rather that criticize yourself for your real or imagined shortcomings. Another way of saying this is to celebrate one's giftedness, skills, strengths, principles rather than lamenting your limitations or weaknesses (your child's too). Please check out an excellent article *Is Your Child 'Normal'?* by Sadhguru in *Khabar Magazine,* February 2016

o   By you sharing when you were a child or now incidents about feelings or handling of situations, the child feels he is not the only one experiencing what he/she is feeling.

o   Listen to your child's fears and happy times, about their day, and what they are interested in, etc. They will be sharing with you who they are.

o   Children go through developmental stages when they are able or not able to do certain tasks. Realize this. Allow your child to act like a child.

 o   Teach yourself and your child about forgiveness: *The Forgiveness Garden* by Tompson, *Forgive and Let Go, A Book About Forgiveness* by Meiners *(Being the Best Me series), Too Many Tamales* by Soto*, The Grudge Keeper* by Rockliff, *God's Dream* by Tutu*, Learning about Forgiveness From The Life of Nelson Mandela, The Story of Mahatma Gandhi* by Logue, *Comments on*

How to Teach a Child Forgiveness by Perillo. Forgive yourself and your child.

o As parents we need to look at the entire picture, like G-d.

o At age two and as a teen, a child will go away from you and then glance back to see if you are still there (for comfort and security).

- I wish parents and many people working with children or writing for children (titles of books) didn't use "kids" for children and young people. "Kids" are baby goats. I personally do not like saying "Kids." I like saying child/children, friends, youth, young people, youngsters, folks, etc. *Please Say Children, Not Kids* by Horvat. For teens another set of words to call them could be "Young People."

- I am trying to stop saying "you guys" for a mixed gender group. Instead I am trying to say "folks" or "youngsters" or "friends."

o *You Guys* by Dr Neal A. Lester, *Teaching Tolerance*, July 9, 2014.

o One of my passions is helping children and adults have "high self-esteem." I believe if one feels good about oneself, when something negative happens, one will be able to deal with it. For example, dealing with bullying, poor grades, etc. One is also more apt to help others when one feels good about oneself.

- Check out these articles:
  Developing Your Child's Self-Esteem
  Kids's Health Narcissistic Kid?
  Blame the Parents by Deborah Netburn
  Science Now, Los Angeles,
  - o "Positive self esteem is important because when people experience it, they feel and look good, are effective and productive, and they respond to others and themselves in healthy, positive, growing ways." by Nathaniel Branden.

o If this interests you as a parent or a teacher, concentrate on repeating many times, "We are a family (classroom) who helps each other" (chores) and /or "brings/builds each other up not tearing/down/teasing."

o Even in the library environment, at the Children's desk, we had one of the "Rules for Fighting Fair" posters that I used with families in "Resolving Family Conflicts." Many patrons commented on them and how helpful they were. Please see Peace Education Foundation Inc., Miami.

o Children need: acceptance, support, encouragement, acknowledgement, recognition, compassion, empathy, acceptance, sensitivity, attention, self-confidence, self-esteem, creativity, a sense of belonging and being treated humanely plus the positive key words below.

o Some positive key words to consider: believe, feel, understand, discover, ascertain, empower, inspire, connect, enrich, energize, creativity, versatile, wonder, awe, passion, vocation, calling, mission, purpose, cause, imagination, curiosity, growth, reach, considerateness, love, openness, nurture, cherish, integrity, dreaming, respect, concern, regard, choice, opportunities, discovery, inspire, motivation, humane, kindness, honesty, gratitude, enlighten, engage, educate, values, ethical, authenticity

o Compromise (give in a little), get together, combine, share, so the situation can turn into a win-win one. Everyone wins when there is cooperation and when children know they will be listened to.

o I believe that both quality time and quantity time are important.

o Playing alone and playing with others have both pluses and minuses and needs to be discussed (role played) with your child.

o "Be a student of your child. Bring out the best in your child. Learn to parent to your child's personality or temperament."

o   Think about you and your child's Birth Order. Check out *The Birth Order Book* by Dr. Kevin Leman. Sometimes we may feel more or less for our child that is in the same birth order we are in. For example, if we were the baby in our family of origin, we may "feel" for our youngest child.

- One of the most common comments I get from parents is how could my two children be so different having been raised by the same parents?
  - The parents are in a different financial place with the second child and in another space as parents, etc.

o   *Parenting-Nature vs. Nurture* by Nina Guilbeau, *Siblings Share Genes, But Rarely Personalities* by Alex Spiegel November 22, 2010, and *Why You and Your Siblings are so Different?* by Perry   Guilbeau, 2010.

o   Change takes time. Be patient with yourself. The only sure thing is change.

o   Use humor but never make fun of anyone (or tease). "Laugh with me, not at me."

  - "When you plant lettuce, if it does not grow well, you don't blame the lettuce. You look for reasons it is not doing well. It may need fertilizer, or more water, or less sun. You never blame the lettuce." by Thich Nhat Hanh (last bullet) There are two ways of looking at this quotation: Putting children into pigeonholes and that they are all the same and taking responsibility for one's actions and not blaming others. This is so hard to teach and to learn even for adults.

- Disguise your voice like a robot, or share a silly voice, etc. Please see *How to Talk So Kids Will Listen* and *Listen So Kids Will Talk* by Faber and Mazlish, page 78. *Encouraging Your Child's Sense of Humor, Where to Draw the Line*

- While on a cruise, I attended a 7:30 pm (usually meaning a Family Friendly show) of a comedian. He was making fun of different cultures. I found it so offensive that I left and I complained to a staff member.
○ Deal with one problem at a time. For example, a child is doing something inappropriate plus name calling. Deal with one situation at a time.
○ Response Able: (responsible) means we are better equipped to respond effectively next time and it is the ability to respond in positive ways to our commitments.
  - "Responsibility is when you see what needs to be done and you do it." *Value Tale, The Value of Responsibility the Story of Ralph Bunche* by Johnson
○ Think about giving a child a promise. I found it better not to promise.
○ It is so important not to judge others and yourself.
○ *Teaching Children to Judge Righteously* by Shannon Symonds
○ Note the following book. *From Myth Busting-Words are Only 7% of our Communication* by Anthony Jacquin.
○ Healthy families communicate.
  - Use active listening skills; share feedback.
  - Rearrange the letters of "silent" and one gets "listen."
  - Notice the difference between lecturing and having a discussion with your family members.
○ Teach kindness by modeling kindness.
  Ask your children and yourself what kind deed did you do today?
  - *Here's How to Raise Kind Kids* by Crain, June 9. 2015,
  - Start a kindness journal sharing what kind deeds you or your child did each day.
  - As a parent, grandparent, teacher, librarian I would often say to the children,"What is the key word? (when it seemed hard to wait). I would respond, "Patience."

- Please note the moving song, *Cats in a Cradle* by Harry Chapin. Songwriters
Chapin, Harry F/Chapin, Sandy
Published by:
Lyrics © Warner/Chappell Music, Inc.
- "Self-discipline means taking ownership, accountability and responsibility for our behavior" by Robert Brooks
o What are your thoughts about this African proverb, "It takes a village to raise a child" or do you feel families raise children? There is also a book by this title by Hillary Clinton and an article *Raising Kids* by Mike Thundering Turtle Ondesko, *Sacred Earth Ways* about this topic.
o I believe people are not "bad." They may do "bad," hurtful things.
o Agreements provide guidance vs rules. Check out *The Four Agreements* by Don Miguel Ruiz and *Ten Powerful Things to Say to Your Ki*ds*: Creating the small relationship you want with the most important people in your life* by Paul Axtell. July 9, 2014.
o "The way we are treated as small children is the way we will treat ourselves and others the rest of our lives: with tenderness and support, with neglect and cruelty, or with something in between." *Hunches on Childhood or Everything I Want to Say About World Peace* by Kent Hoffman.
I believe our goal as parents and educators is to help our children learn from within: learning and having self-discipline, self-regulating, self-control, the reward being what we have learned (reading, a new task, etc.).
Robert Brooks
- I think it is quite important to have self-discipline and get validation/compliments from oneself, not from outer rewards. We need to help our child develop inner discipline and not need outside incentives/bribes, etc. to complete tasks, etc. This is not easy, though.
o *Six Reasons Rewards Don't Work* by Dr. Curwin

o   I believe it is important to take responsibility for ones actions and not scapegoating out to other people.
o   We sometimes would rather say something that could be harmful to our children so that others think we are being a "good parent." We may act kinder towards strangers than our children. Our children seem to be able to push our buttons to such an extreme that we become so very angry.
   ▪ *Treat Your Family Like Strangers* by Heiliger

Unstructured Play

I believe that "unstructured play" is so important with no adults telling children what and how to do something. *The Value of Unstructured Play Time for Kids* by Tom Jacobs, 2014
   ▪ Two books on this topic include: (what a great title – the first one is) *Einstein Never Used Flashcards: How Our Children Really Learn and Why They Need to Play More and Memorize Less* by Dr. Kathy Hirsh-Pasek (co-author) and *The Overscheduled Child* by Alvin Rosenfeld, M.D. (co-author)
   ▪ Through the years, I have found that children have different needs including play and talking and being listened to. Some need more quiet time than others. Some enjoy being busy. Some like doing one activity, whereas others enjoy trying out different activities.
   ▪ "Play is the highest expression of human development in childhood for it alone is the free expression of what is in a child's soul." Friedrich Froebel
   ▪ "Play is the highest form of research." Albert Einstein
   ▪ *Time to Play* by Mothes interviews Kim Hunter about her film *Time to Play, Lilipoh*, Summer, 2015, pages 65-67. (a *Waldorf* teacher)
   Play can be extended and encouraged when your child has friends over. As a young child, when my daughter played with friends, I said watching VHSs were not an option. I had

parents tell me that when they picked up their child from our house, they knew they would be sitting down to see a "play" the children had made up. We had a trunk full of costumes, props, etc. for my daughter and now for my grandson ("Like Paper Bag Dramatics"). Check out My Book, *Education in Different Environments,* under Libraries for more information on this *program.*

The parents would tell us how creative the plays were. Some articles on this topic. *Facilitating Working Play for the Young Child* by Blanning, *Lilipoh,* Summer, 2015, pages 68-69. (a *Waldorf* teacher)

Not Enough Play Time? Journal of Pediatrics

"Playworks was started in 1996 to prevent the sort of fights and disruption at recess" that sometimes happen. *Ban on Tag* by Schouten, *Christian Science Monitor,* 9/15. *Leveling the Playing Field: Building Forts and Building Friendships* by Miller, *The Jewish Georgian* July-August 2015, page 16.

It is believed that students who play well together learn well together.

Adult Led Sports For Children

I believe children don't need to be on sports teams too early. *Pushing Too Hard Too Young, Take Away the Fun Factor in Sports and Children Can Burn Out*, by Jacqueline Stenson, 2004, MSNBC.

Parents and Children's Sports: *Negative Effects of Parents that Push Their Children Into Playing Sports* by Baldwin Ellis, August 16, 2013. *Prevention*

6 Surprising Sports Parent Sins by Cohn, June 23, 2015 *Yahoo Parenting.*

I believe we need to allow our children to have free play and play sports with their own rules and no adult component.

Unstructured Time

I think that it is important for all of us, adults and children, to have "unstructured time" for that is when creativity, and ideas come to you. Daydreaming or staring out the window can be the prerequisite to coming up with a brilliant idea or not so brilliant idea.

Plus when children are so involved with many after-school activities there is no time for unstructured play and just doing nothing (being bored and from that comes imagination and creativity).

"It is precisely the quiet time in stillness, of nothingness that stimulates ideas of nothingness that stimulates ideas. They intrude themselves into the idle moments of relaxation. Without the boredom/relaxation/time wasted, creativity CANNOT exist. Creativity is the residue of time wasted." Albert Einstein

Have some "unscheduled time" when all you do is nothing and just dream. That is when imagination can take over.

The Importance of Doing Nothing by Betsy Brown

Peter Sheras, PhD, clinical psychologist at the University of Virginia, talks about the need for children to have unstructured time to recover from the more structured part of their day and to just veg out. My question is does that mean mineless TV???

Dan Rees, PhD at Western Maryland College says that children who amuse themselves (play) actually exercise a different section of their brain than when they're occupied in something organized.

While I worked at a Florida library, one of my coworkers and I, when we saw each other running around like crazy, would remind ourselves to *Breathe*. This is excellent for children also. Encourage them to breathe. Often during **Story Time**, I would stop the class and ask everyone to take a deep breathe. It works. (Thanks, Ellen)

- Why are we so busy? I want to encourage you to read the fascinating article, *The Disease of Being Busy* by Omid Safi.
- One part of this article talks about asking people how is your heart doing at this very moment? I shared this at a Parenting Support Group and people loved it and wanted to share it with others. People's comments on this article are interesting to read also.
  - *Hands Free Mama* by Stafford

The following **Mrs. Marks' Sparks** are based on the information in *Between Parent and Child* by Dr. H. Ginott and *How To Talk So Kids Will Listen and Listen So Kids Will Talk, Siblings Without Rivalry,* and *Liberated Parents, Liberated Children* all by Adele Faber and Elaine Mazlish. Many of the words/quotes by these authors have helped me and the parents I have worked with.

- When children are in the midst of strong emotions, they cannot listen to anyone (especially in logical terms). Aren't adults like that too? When children get upset, they cannot be reached by reasoning. They want us to understand what is going on inside of them, what they are feeling at that particular moment. They need emotional balm. Feelings must be dealt with before behavior can be improved (acknowledgement). Respond to their upset feelings, rather than to the irritating behavior. At another time, define the problem and together suggest possible solutions (brainstorming/**Problem Solving**). An empathic response that mirrors to children their upset feelings and expresses the parents' sympathy and understanding is effective in changing children's angry moods. Perhaps, have the child draw his feelings.
- Allow the child to express their feelings and wishes. It is the behavior/action that needs to be controlled. While we may not be free to choose the emotions that arise in

us, we are free to choose how and when to express them (behavior), provided we know what they are. Allow children to have and express their feelings and wishes. It is the resulting behavior/action that needs to be controlled. Share times you had strong emotions and what you did with them as a child and an adult.

- Do not ignore your true feelings from your heart. It's best to be authentic/honest with our feelings with our children (and how you feel). A parent should respect their own limits. We can be a little nicer than we feel, but not much. It is important to accept the reality of our feelings of the moment. Really listen to your and your child's feelings.
- Anger is a feeling that needs to have a way to be expressed. It is not a bad feeling. It is normal to have angry feelings. Anger should be expressed in a way that brings some relief to the parent, some insight to the child and no harmful side effects to either of them. It is what one does with the anger that is important. Share with your child different ways of expressing anger. Release anger in short bursts before it builds into an explosion stating in an "I Statements" one's feelings. For example, "I sense you're angry. If you are angry, tell it to me in words." Show anger, without insult.
  ⁘ He who angers you, controls you.
- Both you and your child have rights. Work on sharing mutual respect towards each other.
- It is okay to disagree. Helpful ways to say this: "You feel one way and I feel another way" or "We feel differently on the subject" or "Your opinion seems true to you." "My opinion is different." "I respect your views, but I have another view" or "Thank you for sharing that information and opinion that is valid to you."
- That was yesterday. Today is today.

- Pick your battles. The balloon story: You go to the park with your child and she sees a red balloon for sale and she wants it. You buy it for her and you tell her you will tie it around her wrist so it will not fly away. She says no and she says she will hold onto it. It does fly away. You have a choice. Buy her another one and tie it around her wrist or don't buy it for her because she didn't listen to you the first time. And then you may have an unhappy child the rest of the day. You decide. Told by Zelda Gross, someone who studied with Dr. Ginott. My husband and I attended a monthly parenting workshop with her.
- In response to your child saying, "I hate you" to you or a sibling, one can say "I didn't like what I just heard. If you're angry about something, tell me about it in another way. Then maybe I can be helpful" or "Can you ask me in another way? I cannot hear you with 'That voice'" (whining).
- Siblings don't need to be treated equally, fairly, or uniformly. They need to be treated uniquely.
- Above all, do no damage. (Dr. H. Ginott)
- Take action. There are times for a parent to act, not react (children going to hurt each other).
- Words have the power to build and energize or to frighten and devastate. Use trust/respect, not fear.
- Don't change a mind, change a mood using humor, change of voice, fantasy, imagination.
- Use Brainstorming/**Problem Solving** and eliciting/getting many possibilities of solutions from the child/teen.

My daughter would say as a teen that many of her friends were getting grounded for doing the same thing week after week while we as a family talked and listened and came up with a mutually agreed solution about differences of opinions and letting her go. For example, staying out past a curfew.

- Mediate between siblings if a problem needs **Problem Solving.**

- By beginning to have good communication skills with your child at a young age, one is more apt to have good communication skills in the teen years. You have a baseline (basis) for communicating with each other. But I believe it is never too late to begin communicating.
- I have thought about how I would feel if someone talked about me and said "She is so shy" with me right there. I would feel so embarrassed. Think about labels/roles. Instead perhaps say, this is what she is feeling right now.
- Labeling can be disabling.
- Differences are not liabilities.
- A parent's responsibility is not to his child's happiness, it's to his character. Our basic direction as parents is to help our children be in charge of themselves (eventually be independent). One of our most important goals is to help our children separate from us parents. Giving autonomy is a way of giving love to your child. We help most by not helping and having children do things for themselves (letting go).
- Offer choices (that you can live with/are acceptable to you). Some examples: "You can play with the ball outside or you can give up the privilege of playing with it. You decide."
- Put something else in the negative's place that the child can do. For example: "Walls are not for drawing on, here's some paper." "People are not for hitting. Here's a ball or a punching clown." "People are not for biting. Here's an apple." "This bed/sofa is not for jumping. Here's a pillow on the floor for jumping on."
    - Using *but* tends to dismiss, diminish or erase all that went before. Instead of saying, "I know how much you hate the thought of having a sitter again, but I need to go to the dentist," say, "I know how much you hate the thought of having a sitter again. The problem is I need to go to the dentist." Please see

How To Talk So Kids Will Listen and Listen So Kids Will Talk by Faber and Mazlish pages 268-269

- *What I Did When My Kid Slapped Me* by Bender
- Authority calls for brevity. Only the weak explain themselves and feel defensive. For parents, explanations are unseemly.
- Constant apologies can be inappropriate but not always. When you make a mistake tell your child you are sorry and then make amends.
- Saying 'I am sorry' is only the first step. The second step is to ask yourself what can be done about the situation (restitution). This is true for adults and children.
- You may have to help your child with apologizing and doing the second step. For example, saying "one needs to behave differently and make some kind of change."
- One can also feel sorry and then say, "I'm sorry" for a situation that you are not involved with. This shows empathy and compassion. For example, "I am sorry that you lost your book." (Thanks, Anne and Devyani)
- Acknowledge, acknowledge, acknowledge (showing empathy and compassion to others). Acknowledging is not agreeing. It's a respectful way of opening a dialogue by taking others' statements seriously. It expresses respect or recognition for a child's opinion. By acknowledging the wish of a child and not getting angry, children may feel more comfortable expressing their feelings. When one is acknowledged one feels validated. This is true for adults also.
- Mutual consent means two people agree to it.
- We treat a child as if he already is what we would like him to become.
- "I cannot ever let you do this." (hit me, hit the dog, hurt someone else or yourself). Dr Ginott says "Children should never be allowed to hit their parents" as it is harmful for

Julienne Marks

both children and parents. Please see *Between Parent and Child* by Dr. Ginott, page 130.

- This is not an option. This not an acceptable way of ...This is not acceptable behavior. You need to make a different choice.
- Do not take away hope or prepare for disappointment. Life can be hard.
- Discuss the problem not the person.
- I believe long term goals are more important than short term goals. This is similar to me as process is more important than the product.
  - I do not believe spanking works in the long term. Think about your goals as parents and as a teacher and do you want short or long term goals accomplished? For example, what happens when you spank a child? Yes, perhaps the short term goal may be that the child stops the behavior. But what about the long term goal you are teaching/what have you taught the child: to be aggressive back, his parent physically hurts him, etc.
  - "When a child hits a child, we call it aggression.
  - When a child hits an adult, we call it hostility. When an adult hits an adult, we call it assault.
  - When an adult hits a child, we call it discipline."

Dr.H.Ginott abundantlifechildren.com/2012/09/1 /quote of-the-week-haim-ginott/

We Know Enough Now to Stop Hitting Our Children, Research on Spanking: It's Bad for all Kids. Hitting Children Undermines Well Being in the Long Term. Psychology Today, September 8, 2013, by Darcia Narvaez, Ph.D.

Time Out

- Please see Faber and Mazlish's book, *How To Talk So Kids Will Listen* and *Listen So Kids Will Talk,* about Time Out pages 271-272.
  Also see the following articles on time out.
- *The Disadvantages of Time-Out* by Dr. Aletha Solter
  The Case Against Time-Out by Peter Haimn
  The Art of Mothering, May/June 1998

Meltdowns/Tantrums

Some material on these topics:
- Please see Faber and Mazlish's book, *How To Talk So Kids Will Listen and Listen So Kids Will Talk* about Tantrums. pages 30-32, 40, 45, 128, 163, 291, 292-93
- Tantrums and Meltdowns are defined here. *Why Do Kids Have Tantrums and Meltdowns? Like a fever, these behaviors may have many triggers* by Miller, *Child Minds Institute*
- *Managing the Meltdown* by Lehman

Ideas for a Child Rich Environment

Make your children's room/area, a warm, nurturing, and interesting one for your particular child or children. Get suggestions from the child for his/her room or classroom. When someone contributes or puts in their opinions, one is more apt to want to follow the rules, keep it clean, etc. **(Problem Solving** or brainstorming).

Have a place for the child's work to be displayed: For example, in a child's room or playroom, have a bulletin board so they can put up their awards, artwork, etc. Include display options for projects, collections, and artwork.

White boards or blackboards also can come in handy for leaving notes to oneself. Have some comfortable chairs or places one can lie on the floor with pillows and read or do some work.

In a child's room, have a work place where children can do their work. I do not only mean for homework but a space for individual projects on their passions, interests, and hobbies (for example, Jigsaw puzzles). It is also important to have a space/table that doesn't need to be cleaned up for ongoing projects or board games. Some projects need to be stopped in the middle and then one goes back to it at another time.

What do you do with all the child's 'Work?' The following author has some great ideas. *Sorting and Storing your Child's Artwork* by Robledo in *Real Simple.*

Some children also love stuffed animals.

Following are three articles about creating more nurturing environments for children.

Creating More Nurturing Environments for Children
by Pam Leo

That Tree Used to be Everything to Us: The Importance of Natural and Unkempt Environments to Children by Nicola Ross, Glasgow Centre for the Child & Society, University of Glasgow

Seen and Heard: Some Ideas for Creating a More Child-Friendly Society by Wendy Ponte, *Mothering* September October 1999

I remember around the block from my childhood home was a vacant lot. We would play, ride our bikes through it, (Those bumps of tree roots were great!), and meet our friends there. I have very fond memories of that vacant lot. Other memories I have are playing running bases with my family, playing with the neighborhood children in the backyards, and my father teaching me how to ride a bike on the street next to my home. And the joy and pride I felt when I did it. (Thanks, Dad)

Additional information about the topics in this **Chapter** can be found on the following websites:

files.eric.ed.gov/fulltext/ED496343.pdf.
http://www.med.umich.edu/yourchild/topics/tv.htm
AAP 2001/13, CPS 2010
www.aap.org/.../Pages/Media-and-Children.aspx
http:// www .huffingtonpost.com/2013/09/04/ways-screens-are-ruining-your-familys-life_n_3860927.html
http://www.medialit.org/how-teach-media-literacy
http://pbskids.org/dontbuyit/advertisingtricks/foodadtricks.html
http://www.lyricszoo.com/marlo-thomas/housework-carol-channing/
http://www.npr .org/2015 /09/26/443480452/making-the-case-for-face-to-face-in-an-era-of-digital-conversation
http://wwwnydailynews.com/life-style/health/ipad-bad-children-experts-debate-merits-kids-spending-time-tablets-ipods-article- 1054449#ixzz2oFNKoqTV
http://www.goodreads.com/author/quotes/47146.AlbertSchweit-zer
www.little things.com/...dinner-dads-reaction-priceless
www.screenfree.org
http://movingtolearn.ca/2014/ten-reasons-why-hand-held-devices-should-be-banned-for-children-under-the-age-of-12.
http://en.wikipedia.org/wiki/Character_education
http://eartheasy.com/blog/2011/12/why-eating-family-meals-together-is-still-important-today/
www.rosarygraphics.com
http://www.med.umich.edu/yourchild/topics/tv.htm

Julienne Marks

http://www.huffingtonpost.com/2009/10/26/baby-einstein-refund-get-_n_334068.html
http://www.npr.org/2015/09/26/443480452/making-the-case-for-face-to-face-in-an-era-of-digital-conversation
http://cnnpressroom.blogs.cnn.com/2015/09/10/cnns-anderson-cooper-360-breaks-news-about-teens-and-social-media-in-provocative
http://articles.chicagotribune.com/1995-10-22/news/9510220060_1_child-dear-abby-taught
http://www.riverdale.k12.oh.us/CharacteristicsofGiftedChildren.aspx
http://positiveboomer.net/im-special/
www.pinnacleminds.sg/the-idea-of-multiple-intelligences-virtual-studying-
http://www.newsforparents.org/expert_I_love_you.html and www.readalouddad.com/.../why-parents-should-stop-saying-i-love.htm
www.nbcnews.com/id/.../pushing-too-hard-too-young/
https://www.yahoo.com/parenting/6-surprising-sports-parent-sinszonein.ca
http://www.huffingtonpost.com/lisa-rinkus/call-me-mean-maybe-why-i-wont-get-a-smartphone-for-my-te
http://www.popsugar.com/moms/Children-Feel-Parents-Spend-Too-Much-Time-Devices-37897454
http:// www .huffingtonpost.com/2013/09/04/ways-screens-are-ruining-your-familys-life_n_3860927.html
http:// commercialalert.org/
http://www.medialit.org/how-teach-media-lit eracy
http://pbskids.org/dontbuyit/advertisingtricks/foodadtricks.html
http://www.lyricszoo.com/marlo-thomas/housework-carol-channing/
www.aap.org// Pages/Media-and-Children.aspx
http://pediatrics.aapublications.org/content/119/1/182.full
http://www.quotegarden.com/butterflies.html

https://experiencelife.com/article/walking-your-talk-the-path-of–personal-integrity/

http://www.goodreads.com/quotes/26221-we-teach-best-what-we-most-need-to-learn

http://www.planetofsuccess.com/blog/2012/when-a-door-closes-a-window-opens/

http://www.natashascafe.com/html/cards/card115.html

http://books.simonandschuster.com/AVaueTalesTreaury/SpencerJohnson/9781416998389#sthash.f1NYk8Ra.dpuf or

http://www.valuetales.com/

www.values.com

http://www.values.com/inspirational-stories-tv-spots/

http://www.ehow. com /about_6469084 _difference-silver-rule-golden-rule_.html

http://kidzclub.zaxbys.com/ for-parentand.

https://chick-fil-a kids club .com.

www.mominchapelhillnc.com/2011/05/chick-fil-a-mom-valet.html

http://eatocracy.cnn.com/2014/05/15/chipotle-aims-to-cultivate-thought-on-its-packaging/

http://kdhnews.com/blogs/savealotmom/chilis-daddy-daughter-night-out-check-this-out/article_67cd1dfc-1442-11e5-9b53-5b5a6fedc6f1.html

www.goodreads.com//394286-there-are-no-mistakes-only-o

http://boardofwisdom.com/togo/Quotes/ShowQuote?msgid=4631

https://charactercounts.org/resources/index.htm3#.VpKLZU-Number 49: Spring 2015. "Teaching Tolerance"

http://www.tolerance.org /magazine/ number-49-spring-2015/feature/learning-begood?elq Track Id=0C7D7E7B82538FAC27AF4B0BFC3CFCCA&elq =fac3fc4ab2574e60a21fd21e240f0f3c&elqCampaignId=477& elqaid=515&elqat=1o2ZY

http://www.finweb.com/financial-plan ning/teach-your-kids-to-give-and-spend-wisely.htlm# ixzz381GO900

http://www.huffingtonpost.com/fatherly-/why-danish-parents-and-th_b_8106792.html?ncid=txtlnk usa olp

0http://www.chick-fil-a.com/Story/Detail/6094 0000592&ref=yfp

http://familyshare.com/helping-your-children-find-their-passions

http://www.cleveland. com/ parents/index.ssf/2015/04/helicopter_vs_free-rangehow a.html

http://www.theatlantic.com/features/archive/2014/03/hey-parents-leave-those-kids-alone/358631/

http://www.parents.com/parenting/better-parenting/ what-is-helicopter-parenting/

http://the familydinnerproject.org/resources/faq/

http://childdevelopmentinfo.com/parenting /the-importance-of-teaching-manners-to-kids/

http://peaceinyourhome.com/should-parents-pay-kids-allowance-for-chores/

http://blog.positivediscipline.com/2014/01/a-misbehaving-child-is-discouraged-cwww.scoutsongscom/ lyrics/little-bunny-foo-foo.html

hild.html#sthash.wrO3gFYY.dpufPositive

http://www.quotesigma.com/best-african-proverbs-2/

www.ifyoulovetoread.com/book/chten cats 1105 .htm

www.topics-mag.com/edition11/games-section.htm and

Circle Games: www.ultimatecampresource.com/site/camp/ circle-games.page-4.html

www.cntraveler.com/.../Around-the-World-in-50

www.fabermazlish.com

http:/ /www.askdrsears.com/ topics/parenting /discipline.behavior/moralsmanners/why-do-kids-lie

http://www.childmag. co.za/content/what-white-lies-teach-your-

www. affirmationsforpositivethinking.com
www.brainyquote.com/quotes/quotes/v/virginiasa175185html
http://start withyourstrengths.com/
http://psychcentral.com/blog/discuss/42236/psychcentral.com/.../02/27/how-to-teach-a-child-Forgiveness
http://www.traditioninaction.org/Cultural/C023cpKids.htm.
http://www.tolerance.org /blog/ you-guys
http://kidshealth.org/parent/ emtions/feelings/self_esteem.html
www.mdjunction.com /.../positive .../3619067-the -importance-of-self-esteem.
http://www.peace education .org /html
http://www.bellaonline.com/articles/art13247.asp
theparentingpassageway.com/2010/05/28/the-four-temperaments
http://www.npr.org/2010/11/18/131424595/siblings-share-genes-but-rarely-personalities.
http://www.minnpost.com/second-opinion/2010   /12/why-you-and-your-siblings-are-so-different
http://familyshare.com/teaching-children-to-judge -righteously
http://tenpowerfulthingstosaytoyour kidsTumblr.com
http://www.metrolyrics.com/cats-in-the-cradle-lyrics-harry-chapin.html
http://www.parenthood.com/article/how_to_teach_kids_selfdiscipline.html#.VVynqFJh
http //www.edutopia.org/blog/reward-fraud-richard-curwin
http://metothepowerofwe.com/featured-quote/be-polite-and-kind/
http://www.psmag.com/navigation/books-and-cultre/value-unstructured-play-time-kids-81177/.
http://www froebel.web.org/web7001.html
http://www.goodreads.com/quotes/286612-play-is-the-highest-form-of-research
http:// news.yahoo.com/ban-tag-school-children-getting-playtime-192828254.html
www.atlantajewishtimes.com December 11, 2015, page 23

http://www.live strong .com/article/523031-negative-effects-of-parents-that-push-their-children-into-playing-sports/

http://www.scholastic.com/parents/resources /article/creativity-play/joys-doing-nothing

http://parentingwithunderstanding.com/2012/01/03/long-term-not-short-term-goals/

http://www.aware parenting.com/timeout.htm

http://www.childmind.org/en/posts/articles/2013-10-29-why-do kids-

http://www.empoweringparents.com/managingmeltdown.php#i xzz3ea8a8rWz

http://www.realsimple.com/work-life/family/kids-parenting/sorting-storing -childs-artwork

http://www.naturalchild.org/guest/pam_leo3.html

http://www.openspace.eca.ac.uk/conference/proceedings/PDF/Ross.pdf

Child-Friendly Initiative www.childfriendly initiative.org

https://starlightworker.wordpress.com/-to-really-listen-rearrange-the -letters.

Yahoo Parenting

thesunmagazine.org/issues/150.at pediatrics.aappulbications.org

Braun on Mar.19, 2010

http://betsybrownbraun.com/2010/03/19/the-importance-of-doing-nothing/

http://betsybrownbraun.com/2010/03/19/the-importance-of-doing-nothing/

e/http://www.artadvice.com/blog/2012/07/01/the-importance-of-wasting-tim

www.onbeing.org/blog/the –disease-of being –busy/7023.

www.handsfreemama.com another interesting article on this topic.

Another take on your older children's 'treasures.' smallnote-book.org/.../your-childs-keepsakes-30-years-later.

us.macmil -lan.com/dountootters/LaurieKeller.
religions kidworldcitizen.org/2014/ .../ world-religions-golden-rule-across-cultures/
http://www.moralstories.org/learning-from-mistakes/
http://thinkexist.com/quotation/you_see_things-and_you_say--why-but_i_dream/13471.htmlhttp://www.authentic-self.com/authentic-self-quotes.html.
www.businessdictionary.com/definition/values.html
http://www.ouroutofsynclife.com/2010/12/today-by-henry-matthew-ward.html
fun.familyeducation.com
www.khabar.com/magazine/spiritual-straight-talk/is-your-child-normal
http://psychcentral.com/blog/discuss/42236/psychcentral.com/.../02/27/how-to-teach-a-child-Forgiveness.
www.quoteland.com/author/Thich-Nhat-Hanh-Quotes/1758/
spotlightenglish. Com /listen/purposely-imperfect.
http://www.natashascafe.ucom/html/cards/card115.html
http://boardofwisdom.com/togo/Quotes/ShowQuote?msgid=43 6313#.VpKLZU-o2ZY
http://kids health.org/parent/growth/learning/childhumor html#a_Where_to_Draw_the_Line

Chapter 5

GRANDPARENTING

Quotations

"I used to think I was too old to fall in love again, but then I became a grandma." Anonymous

"When a child is born so is a grandmother." Judith Levy

"What children need most are the essentials that grandparents provide in abundance. They give unconditional love, kindness, patience, humor, comfort, lessons in life. And, most importantly, cookies." Rudolph Giuliani

"Being grandparents sufficiently removes us from the responsibilities so that we can be friends." Dr. Allan Fromme

"Who are we, if we are not who we are." Ethan Greenfield, my grandson, November 4, 2015

GENERAL INFORMATION ABOUT THE AUTHOR AND GRANDPARENTING

Being a grandparent is fabulous. When you talk to other grandparents, most people agree. There is something so wonderful spending time with your grandchild. It is also very special watching your child with your grandchild. You can share who you are with your grandchild. Love is what it is all about.

Many people have talked to me about spoiling children both due to having an only child and being a grandparent. I am quite aware of this. I do believe in "spoiling" with attention, time and experiences but not with things.

I also think it is important to share with your grandchildren about getting older in mind and body. For example, one time I picked up my grandson an hour earlier from school than I was supposed to. I was embarassed but we talked about it and played outside really enjoying ourselves for that extra hour. I tell my grandson about a memory course I once took. The speaker talked about file cabinets in our minds. Children can picture themselves having one file cabinet in their mind that holds all the information they know and have learned. Grandparents and older people, who have lived a long time, have many file cabinets in their mind and when they are asked a question or need to think of a word, it has to go through many file cabinets to come to the answer. That is why it may take us longer to get an answer. I find that the less I worry about not knowing/having the word or answering immediately, the faster it will come to my mind.

My grandson would ask me about a feeling he may be having and say, "Have you ever felt this way, MA?" I feel sharing feelings and incidents that have happened to us, with our grandchildren, is extremely important. The child then, doesn't feel he/she is alone with these feelings. My daughter and my grandson have taught be so much.

Try these articles.

- *Grandparents A Critical Link to Your Children's Future* by Patricia Fry
- *How to Be a Grandparent: 8 Lessons I Learned From My Grandparents* by Kelle Hampton
- *Grandparents Role in the Family*

Julienne Marks

A Talk with Grandparents

I gave this talk to a group of Grandparents. My goal was to share several books about Grandparents that are fun and also through books show how we grandparents can share some of our traditions, religions, values, and what our role is to our grandchildren. Although I am focusing on books with the theme of grandparents, books of all themes and topics can be read to/with your grandchild.

A Sample of items I talked about at "A Talk with Grandparents." Some of these items could also be used during "Grandparent **Story Time**" or "Grandparent Connection Time" below.

- Read to very young children.

Mother Goose Rhymes are so important due to their sound and the rhythm.

- Even when your grandchildren are reading, keep reading to them.
- Nonfiction books on subjects your grandchild is interested in can be encouraged even when the child is very young, especially ones with great pictures and photographs.
- Turn off the computer, cell phone, TV and DVD's, iPad. There are negative studies even about Baby Einstein. Please note information in **Chapter 4** on Technology, under Talks.
- Play music, color, paint, have available a sand box (In the winter try using oatmeal).
- Young children may enjoy playing with water. Put a few cups, etc. in the sink and let the children play. (Thanks, Aunt Joannie)
- Have items in your pocketbook for your grandchild. For example, string for *Cat's In A Cradle*, playing cards, paper and crayons, books, puppets, etc. (Parents, you too.) This

can actually came in handy on an airplane ride for a child whose ears are hurting.

- Do something special each year (a tradition).
- Give special meaningful gifts (that have some *connection*). As a parent I would give my daughter a looking-at "non playing" good doll for her birthday. She had other dolls to play with. She now has some collection. Books in a *series* are another idea.
- Leave a recording or written book about your life. I am using for my grandson a book which was given to me by my daughter: AARP's *For my Grandchild, A Grandmother's Gift of Memory*. My daughter and daughter-in-law gave me *My Quotable Grandkid* by Chronicle Books.
  - For your child you can also prepare a Parent's Book. For example *For My Children: A Mother's Journal of Memories, Words, and Wisdom* by Dionna Ford.
- Share some of your Family Stories. Please see later on in this **Chapter** for information.
- If you are not a Grandparent or your grandchildren aren't near where you live, find some children who need a Grandparent.
- Examples of "Interviewing Questions" children can ask their Grandparents (to tape, write down, or just listen to). Choose the ones that appeal to you.

  - Are there any special stories about your family you want to share when you were growing up?
  - What were your parents, grandparents like? Were they born in the United States?
  - Talk about your brothers and sisters or if you are an only child, what was that like for you growing up?
  - What was the name of your best friend?
  - Do you remember any teachers you would like to tell me about?

- Did you ride a bicycle when you were a child? Who taught you how to ride?
- What scared you as a child?
- What was one of your happiest moments?
- What was one of your saddest moments?
- What were some of your favorite music groups, favorite plays, or favorite books?
- What things do we have today that were not in existence when you were young?
- How did you like to celebrate your birthday?
- Have you ever traveled to another country and what was it like?
- If you could travel in a time machine and go back in history what time period would you choose? Who would you like to meet? Have dinner with?
- Is there any particular event you would like to have witnessed?
- What two things would you like to learn how to do and why?
- When has been the best time of your life and why?
- ❖ My Mom would always say when we children asked her this question, "It is whatever time I am in now." (Thanks, Mom)
- What was the biggest change in your life during the past year?
- What is the most important spiritual/religious thing you want to share with me?
- What qualities do you think make lifelong friends?
- How did you meet your husband/wife, other grandparent/spouse?
- Tell about the child's Mom/Dad when she/he was growing up.
- What is the last grade in school you went to?
- What do you remember about the different seasons? For example in the winter, was it very cold when you were

little? Was it freezing? Did you play in the snow and on the ice? Did you ice skate, go sledding, build a snowman?

+ What are some of your favorite memories?

+ What are some of your hobbies?

+ What would be a perfect day for you?

+ Is there anything else you would like to share with me about when you were growing up?

+ What were some of the greatest challenges in your work?

+ Did you ever volunteer? If so, what did you do? What was it like?

+ Have you accomplished what you wanted to in life?

+ What words do you live by or are very important to you?

+ What advice would you like to give me?

+ How do you relax?

+ If you found a magic lamp with a Genie who would grant you three wishes, what would they be?

+ Talk about what are some of your favorite/least favorite foods.

+ When you are having a bad day, what's the best thing you do to cheer yourself up?

+ When you see someone sad, what do you do to help them feel better?

+ What is the best gift you have ever received?

+ Share some special stories about my Mom/Dad when they were growing up.

Following are some books I shared during the Talks and **Story Time** for Grandparents and Grandchildren

Grandma by Bailey (board book)

Grandma's Beach by Beardshaw (Going to an imaginative beach)

Grandma According to Me by Beil

Something to Remember Me By by Bosak

Julienne Marks

When You Visit Grandma and Grandpa by Bowen (Teaching a younger sibling what to expect)
Grandmother and I by Buckley (African American; lap)
Grandfather and I by Buckley (African American; walk slowly)
A Day's Work by Bunting (Hispanic, not telling the truth)
I Have an Olive Tree by Bunting (Greek)
Sunshine Home by Bunting (Nursing home)
At Grandpa's Sugar Bush by Carney (Tradition of making maple syrup)
Big Mama's by Crews (African American; tradition of summer)
Abuela by Dorros (Hispanic American; flying and using your imagination over New York City)
How Does it Feel to be Old? by Farber
The Patchwork Quilt by Flournoy (African American; quilt)
Something From Nothing by Gilman (Jewish Folktale, tailor)
Sunrise, Sunset by Harnick (Jewish family in Russia; all about families)
The Friday Nights of Nana by Hest (Jewish Celebration of Shabbat with extended family.
Spot Visits his Grandparents by Hill (find hidden things)
38 Ways to Entertain Your Grandparents by Hunter
When I Am Old With You by Johnson (African American)
The Hello Goodbye Window by Juster (Caldecott winner for artwork)
Let's Talk About Living with a Grandparent by Kent
Ultimate Guide to Grandmas and Grandpas by Lloyd-Jones
I Go With My Family to Grandma's by Levinson (1920s in Manhattan traveling to Grandma's)
Across the Alley by Michelson (African American; Jewish American; prejudice; Holocaust)
The Keeping Quilt by Polacco (Jewish immigration; generations; quilt)

142

Mrs. Katz and Tush by Polacco (African American child and Jewish widow)
When Jo Louis Won the Title by Rochelle (African American; immigrate from the South; how grandparents met; child's name)
Grandfather's Journey by Say (Caldecott winner for artwork; Japanese American; immigration)
Gran's Bees by Thompson (granddaughter and grandmother share love of Bees)

Everyone's story is important

Family Stories

Family Stories are what one remembers through the years. Besides the above interview questions, sharing Family Stories (parents also) about your life as children or how sharing your important decisions both positive and negative can help children to see the continuity of life.

I believe that Family Stories are a gift you can share/give to your children/grandchildren and are very important. I find the following quite interesting. A child knowing about his family history (through interviews of family members, family stories, etc.) helps to build the resiliency of the child. *The Stories that Bind* by Bruce Felier which is adapted from his book, *The Secrets of Happy Families: How to Improve Your Morning, Rethink Family Dinner, Fight Smart, Go Out and Play, and Much More.*

For more information on resiliency please note *Building Resilience in Children,* American Academy of Pediatrics.

I also attended a class about Family Stories which was quite informative.

Julienne Marks

A Few of My Family Stories

More of my Family Stories are found throughout this book. To give you some examples, here are a few of my Family Stories.

I love how I received my name. My grandfather (my mother's father) would sign his checks Jullian, J the initial for Joseph and Ullian his last name. My mother told the nurse when she was asked what my name would be Jullian. But the nurse wrote on the birth certificate: Julienne.

We had always celebrated my birthday on October 13. When my family of origin went to Niagara Falls we needed our birth certificates. My birth certificate stated I was born on October 14. All those years we had celebrated it on October 13. What it was was that when I was born, October 12 (Columbus Day) was on a Sunday but celebrated on Monday (October 13). My father therefore thought it was the 13 (the day after Columbus Day) but in actuality it was October 14. My siblings call me every year on October 13 and say which day is it anyway the 13 or the 14? In fact in writing this, I became confused again.

During that same time when we were at Niagara Falls, my sisters looked at their birth certificates. Previously, we had been told that Marsha was 20 minutes older. But the birth certificates said the reverse. We were never sure about this one.

Ethan spoke "Papa" first for my husband. Finally he called me "MA" because my daughter would call me Ma so he picked that up.

I had an older cousin who would babysit. He would share a story using my name in it. It went like this. Once upon a time there was a little girl, named Julienne whose cousin (Barry) came to babysit her. She asked him to tell her a story and this is the story he told her. There was a little girl named Julienne whose cousin (Barry) came to babysit her. She asked him for a story and this is the story he told her. And then keep repeating the story over and over again. I loved this story! (Thanks, Barry)

(PR) Public Relations

Grandparent Story Time/Grandparents Connection

Date:
Ages 6 and up
Join us for a special time about Grandparents with music, stories, and poems about Grandparents. If you can, bring your Grandparent or an older friend. Let's celebrate Grandparents.

A Sample of an **Agenda** for a **Grandparent StoryTime/ Gandparent Connection.**

1. Introduce self.
2. Have child introduce their grandparent by saying some thing that makes them special to you. Then have the grandparents share one thing special about their grand-child.
3. Read three books:
   a. *The Ultimate Guide to Grandmas and Grandpas*!
      by Lloyd-Jones
   b. *Something From Nothing* by Gilman
   c. *Gran's Bees* by Thompson
4. Sing (ask for Grandparents' favorites) For example, *I've Been Working on the Railroad, She'll be Coming Round the Mountain, There's a Hole in the Bucket. The Reader's Digest Children's Songbook* (#4) by Simon
5. Up Activities: *Here We Go Loopty Loo.*
6. Play Classical music and move to it.
7. Poetry time: Read a poem about Grandparents.

8. In between one can talk about: what do you call your grandparents?
9. Draw a picture of you and your Grandparent doing something together having fun or making a Family Tree after explaining what a Family Tree is. Or perhaps use different colored stick pins on a map showing where the children's ancestors come from.

Feedback

"The Grandparent Connection" was a good experience for the children to learn things about grandparents, real or borrowed ones. The children present enjoyed hearing from the grandparents things they did growing up. It was interesting to hear the things the children enjoyed doing with grandparents." (a grandparent)

Activities to Do with Grandchildren Near or Far
Here are some sample activities to share with your grandchildren

o Talk about relatives while making a Family Tree. (Genealogy)
o Share who you are and what you like to do: philosophy, hobbies, favorite quotations, traditions, etc.
o Have some special activities you do with your grandchild remembering each grand child is special and unique. One grandma I know cooks all the time with her grandchildren (Thanks, Shelly)
o Send notes/letters/emails to your grandchild.
o Skype
o For older children read the same book your grandchild is reading. Have a discussion on the phone.

o For younger children read a picture book over the phone. I had a friend who read *Brown Bear Brown Bear, What Do You See?* by Carle to her grandchild. (Thanks, Nancy)
o Some more books with ideas and activities for Grandparents
  ▪ *Something to Remember Me* by Susan Bosak
  ▪ *The Really Useful Grandparents' Book* by Eleo Gordon and Tony Lacey
  ▪ *Grandmother's Book* by Parragon Publishers
  ▪ *The Little Big Book for Grandmothers* Edited by Lena Tabori

Older People

This poem really moves me. *What Do You See When You See Me?* (a poem) (A nurse told me that she was shown this poem prior to working with Seniors to encourage compassion) (Thanks, Ginny)

This poem was found among the possessions of an elderly lady who died in the geriatric ward of a hospital. No information is available concerning her — who she was or when she died. Reprinted from the "Assessment and Alternatives Help Guide" prepared by the Colorado Foundation for Medical Care.

There is also a children's book with the same title. *What Do You See When You See Me?* by Jeannie St. John Taylor

Seattle Preschool in a Nursing Home Transforms Elderly Residents by Brown. Watch this and see. It will move you. Why isn't this being done everywhere? It can be wonderful for both children and adults.

I found the following websites helpful:

http://www.thequotepedia.com/i-used-to-think-i-was-too-old-to-fall-in-love-again-but-then-i-became-a-grandma/
thinkexist.com/quotation/being_grandparents_sufficiently
www.coolnsmart.com › Browse Quotes By Grandmother
http://thinkexist.com/quotation/when_a_child_is_born-so_are_grandmothers/210140.html
http://www.notable-quotes.com/g/giuliani_rudolph.html
https://gma.yahoo.com/seattle-preschool-nursing-home-transforms-elderly-residents-201932520--abc-news-parenting.html#
http://www.matilijapress. com/articles /grand parents.htm
Sept. 04, 2014.
http://www.ehow.com/ehow-mom/blog/how-to-be-a-grandparent-8-lessons-i-learned-from-my-grand-parents
/?utm_source=newsletter&utm_medium=email&utm_campaig
n=ehow_general_0911
http://www.a-better-child.org/page/888950
https://www.healthychildren.org/English/healthy-living/ emo-tional-wellness/Building-Resilience/Pages/Building-Resilience-in-Children.aspxes.com/2013/03/17/fashion/the-family-stories-that-bind-us-this-life.html
http://grandparentsday.fundootimes.com/poems/funny-poems.html
http://grandparentsday.fundootimes.com/poems/kids-poems.html
genaloogy.about.com/od/children/Genealogy_for_Children.ht
m   https://images.search.yahoo.com/images/view.
http://www.nursinghomealert.com/share-this-poem

Chapter 6

ADULT ACTIVITIES

Importance of Alone Adult Time

I believe adult time alone is very important for parents, both for yourself and with your spouse or significant other. One can be recharged to be with your children after you have done something for yourself that you enjoy. For example: Take a walk, listen to music you like, take a bubble bath, pet your cat, get out into or observe nature, etc. If I needed some space due to a migraine or I just needed some alone time, I would tell my daughter that she could sit by me coloring or looking at books because I needed to have some quiet time so Mommy would not become irritable.

Finding a trusted Babysitter can be daunting. I wanted an older adult for occasional afternoons and evenings. I wanted someone who would play with my daughter and not watch TV or have my daughter watch TV. I was very clear with my desires. I interviewed, talked, observed and I found Dolores who "played " with Elissa. I was very lucky. Dolores attended many of our family events, for example, the dance recital, Elissa and I were both in. "I so enjoyed watching you on toe at your dance recital." (Thanks, Dolores)

Time with women friends can be so nurturing and rewarding. Check out article *New Mom Friendship.*

Adult time with your spouse is also very important. Make a date monthly and go out and don't talk only about the children. Perhaps even go away. When we first had my daughter we would go away every six months. I was fortunate my Mom or brother could come to be with our daughter. (Thanks Mom and Bill) My husband and I would be able to prioritize our goals for the next few months when we went away and concentrated on "us."

Date nights, vacations, weekends away (some without) are important for married couples. My parents would go away once a year on a vacation just for them and another vacation with us children.

My husband and I also experienced several "Marriage Encounter" weekends. A Marriage Encounter weekend is a time to concentrate on your marriage. It is a weekend to "be" and share who you really are with your spouse.

We were taught to *communicate* with each other during and after the weekends and thus to continue working on our relationship. There are different Marriage Encounters by location and religion. For more information, put in Google "Marriage Encounter" and your nearest city. (Thanks, Pat and Sam for asking us to trust you and all the people we met through Marriage Encounter.)

Adult Birthday or Other Celebrations (Milestones) Ideas

When we decided to move from New York to Florida we gave ourselves a goodbye party.

I gave myself my own 40th birthday party, invited old and new friends, full of cake, reminiscences, etc. My Mom came in from California which made it extra special.

When I turned 50, I sent a letter to all my friends, old and new, and asked them to send me a letter telling about a time we were together that was meaningful to them; a memory. I received this idea from my sister-in-law who also did it for my brother. A new friend took the idea and for her mother's birthday did something similar. I received many interesting and meaningful times from my life. I also heard from many people whom I hadn't heard from in a long time. I put all these letters in a notebook and I often look at them. I actually received one from a former student who was in graduate school studying to become a teacher (I had been her second grade teacher) who said she so remembered me and hoped to be a teacher like me someday. On her application when it asked why did she want to be a teacher, she said to be like me! You can imagine how I felt.

The first time I became a Librarian II, I gave myself a party celebrating my promotion.

For my 60th birthday I asked friends for a quotation, prayer, or story that was meaningful to them to share with me. I received so many wonderful ones. I also put these into another notebook. For example: "So live that G-d could publish a book about you and you would not be ashamed for the whole world to read it." Warren Wiersbe (Thanks, Mae)

When we moved into our second apartment and then our home in Georgia, we gave ourselves housewarming parties.

When I turned 65 I again gave myself a Party. I asked the people I invited to write a memory of us together. This was a new set of friends as I had moved to Georgia and now I had another notebook. For example, "I loved watching you work on and perform your ballet dance, *Canon in D Major* by Pachelbel." (Thanks, Jackie) (Another time I learned this piece by piano. It is one of my brother's favorite pieces of music.)

When I was leaving a workplace I asked staff and patrons, including children I had worked with, to write some memories they had of us together:

I was given three lovely goodbye parties at three Florida Libraries, and a retirement party at a Georgia library (Thanks, Mona, Andy, Cindi, Jo, and Roxanne)

I had been at a library for eight years. Then I left to work at a library nearer to my home and for fewer hours. I received some wonderful memories which I also put into another notebook. For example, "I will treasure our talks about Homeschooling, peace education, and life and all of your support." (Thanks, Barbara)

When I retired and left another library I had been at for five years and five months, I again asked staff and patrons, including children I had worked with to write some memories. I again received some wonderful memories which I also put into another notebook. For example, "You are so much fun to talk books with. Thanks for all the book recommendations." (Thanks, Megan)

Think about ideas you would like to do to celebrate the milestones in your life.

Feedback

"You are a great event planner. You plan special events at your home where people can enjoy being with one another. From housewarmings, to a Woman's group where women's issues are discussed to birthday parties, you plan and present social events where one feels welcome and special." (Library Director) (Thanks, Helen) Please see my Book, *Education in Different Environments,* under Networking for more information on Women's Group.

Some helpful websites on this topics in this **Chapter**:

https://www.care.com/a/revitalize-date-night-1011091118 , http://www.popsugar.com/moms/Vacation-Without-Kids-28964092

Chapter 7

RESOURCES

What I have shared with you in this Book is a combination of ideas gleaned through the years from books, quotations, articles, and families, parents, grandparents, and children I have met and worked with. Books such as the following:

How Does Your Child Grow? by Edna Le Shan
Living, Loving, and Learning by Leo Buscaglia, and others found in this **Chapter** and throughout the Book

Quotations

"Don't spend your precious time asking 'Why isn't the world a better place?' It will only be time wasted. The question to ask is 'How can I make it better?' To that there is an answer." by Leo Buscaglia

Dr. Mother Teresa, who said "Find your Calcutta," *From Happier at Home,* by Rubin, page 228.

Thank you to the Families, Parents, grandparents, and children I have met and worked with. I have tried to give credit to other people's ideas by saying Thanks, and the person's first name.

I like to write letters. I wrote to the following authors and received letters back. Some excerpts from others' letters or emails follow. How thrilling to get letters or emails back from:

Dr. Alice Ginott, clinical psychologist and wife of the late renowned psychologist, Dr. Haim Ginott, who updated *Between Parent and Child* wrote, "Zelda Gross's (My husband and I studied with her in a Parenting Support Group) daughter who was 16 at the time illustrated a pamphlet for me. I am delighted you are sharing workshops based on the Ginott principles of communication."

Adele Faber, author of *How To Talk So Kids Will Listen and Listen So Kids Will Talk* and other books, wrote, "We're delighted by your response to our work, Thank you!"

Dr. Susan Jeffers, author of *Feel the Fear and Do It Anyway* and other books wrote, "Thank you for the many beautiful contributions to this world. I just love what you are doing."

Alfie Kohn, author of *Unconditional Parenting* and other books, wrote, "I appreciate your kind words and am delighted that you will be introducing *Unconditional Parenting* to the parents you work with. Fran Schmidt (author of many Peace Education Foundation Inc., Miami curriculums was my sixth grade teacher and I have been in touch with her a number of times. I was briefly on her Board of Peace Foundation. I am also glad to hear you're encouraging reading rather than undermining interest in it by offering rewards."

"Nice to hear from you again. I'm glad you're in there fighting to help children appreciate reading for its own sake." (Kohn)

Dr. Mel Levine, author of *A Mind at A Time* and other books wrote, "It is obvious that we are on the same 'wavelength.'"

Neil Postman, who wrote *The Disappearance of Childhood* and other books (Please note another book on the same topic: *Loss of Childhood found in Children Without Childhood* by Winn) wrote, "It always gives me great pleasure to hear from former teachers and current librarians for whom my work has some value."

Fred Rogers, author of *You are Special* and other books, wrote, "Your personal and professional support of our work means a great deal to us."

Fran Schmidt, author of many Peace Education curriculums wrote, "I am sending you a free copy of *We Can Work it Out! Building Peace in the Home*. As I honor your opinion, I would like to know what you think of the book."

The following authors called me after they received my letter: Dr Susan Jeffers, Dr. Alice Ginott, and Susan Fitzell. I was so thrilled.

I also spoke to Leslie Faber, Adele Faber's husband who was complementary about my results of using the workshops, *How to Talk So Kids Will Listen™* and *Siblings Without Rivalry™* both by Adele Faber and Elaine Mazlish.

More Books that I have Used

Recommended with Book Descriptions

Here are some of books, especially Parenting Books that I have read and recommended during my *programs* and used throughout my work career. Many of the books already listed throughout this book are not repeated here. Using the Internet and giving the title and author, one can find many of these books on Amazon.

The Hurried Child by David Elkind

Book Description:

"In the third edition of this classic (2001), Dr. Elkind provided a detailed, up-to-the-minute look at the Internet, classroom culture, school violence, movies, television, and a growing societal incivility to show parents and teachers where hurrying occurs and why. And as before, he offered parents and teachers insight, advice, and hope for encouraging healthy development while protecting the joy and freedom of childhood." Amazon.com.

The Power of Play: Learning What Comes Naturally
by David Elkind

Book Description:

"Today's parents often worry that their children will be at a disadvantage if they are not engaged in constant learning, but child development expert David Elkind reassures us that imaginative play goes far to prepare children for academic and social success." Amazon.com

Other books by Elkind include:
Grandparenting: Understanding Today's Children
All Grown Up and No Place to Go
Ties that Stress: The New Family Imbalance
Miseducation: Preschoolers at Risk

Books by Alvyn Freed:

The New TA for Kids and Grown-Ups Too
Powerful Techniques for Developing Self-Esteem
Transactional Analysis for Everyone Series (also *TA for Tots, TA for Teens and Other Important People*)

Book Description:

"*TA for KIDS* is part of the Transactional Analysis for Everybody *Series*. This classic book has proven to be ideal for helping youngsters develop self-esteem, esteem of others, personal and social responsibility, critical thinking and independent judgment." Amazon.com

Frames of Mind: The Theory of Multiple Intelligences
by Howard Gardner

Book Description:

"Gardner's trailblazing book revolutionized the worlds of education and psychology by positing that rather than a single type of intelligence, we have several--most of which are neglected by standard testing and educational methods." Amazon.com

Emotional Intelligence by Daniel Goleman

Book Description:

"In this fascinating book, based on brain and behavioral research, Daniel Goleman argues that our IQ-idolizing view of intelligence is far too narrow. Instead, Goleman makes the case for 'emotional intelligence' being the strongest indicator of human success. He defines emotional intelligence in terms of self-awareness, altruism, personal motivation, empathy, and the ability to love and be loved by friends, partners, and family members. People who possess high emotional intelligence are the people who truly succeed in work as well as play, building flourishing careers and lasting, meaningful relationships. Because emotional intelligence isn't fixed at birth, Goleman outlines how adults as well as parents of young children can sow the seeds." Amazon.com

The Explosive Child by Ross Greene

Book Description:

"Dr. Ross Greene helps you understand why and when your child does these things and how to respond in ways that are nonpunitive, nonadversarial, humane, and effective."
Amazon.com

An Article to share:

The American Education System Completely Misunderstands How to Discipline Children says Groundbreaking Psychologist (Dr. Ross Green) by Weller

Different Learners: Identifying, Preventing, and Treating Your Child's Learning Problems by Dr. M. Healy

Book Description:

"Today's fast-paced, stressed-out culture is hazardous to growing minds, says Healy, and a growing 'epidemic' of children's disorders is the result. *Different Learners* offers a complete program not only for treating the child, but also for making more beneficial lifestyle choices at home and improving teaching techniques at school." Amazon.com

Failure To Connect: How Computers Affect Our Children's Minds And What We Can Do About It
by Dr. M. Healy

Book Description:

"This important book is a welcome addition to the growing (and long overdue) debate about how much of a good thing it is to mix computers and children. For example, what a miracle computers have been for some handicapped children. But her conclusions about the routine use of computer technology in the classroom are overwhelmingly - and persuasively negative." Amazon.com

Other books by Dr. Healy

Your Child's Growing Mind: Brain Development and Learning From Birth to Adolescence

Endangered Minds: Why Children Don't Think And What We Can Do About It

Teach Your Own by John Holt

Book Description:

"This book has helped thousands of people from all over the world to start homeschooling. The timeless insights into how children learn and his perspective on homeschooling as being completely different from just school at home, make this book useful, and important." Amazon.com

For homeschooling parents, this book is a must!
Julienne Marks, the author

Growing Without Schooling by John Holt

Book Description:

"Founded in 1977 by John Holt, *Growing Without Schooling* (GWS) was the first magazine published about homeschooling, unschooling, and learning outside of school."

I received and read every copy of (GWS), eating up the way the parents "taught" their children. It was so enlightening. I lent my copies of GWS out to interested Homeschooling parents (whom I met at the libraries I worked at). The parents really appreciated this. Julienne Marks, the author

Please see My Book, *Education in Different Environments*, about Homeschooling.

Some Books by Alfie Kohn:

Unconditional Parenting
Moving from Rewards Punishment to Love and Reason

Book Description:

"Most parenting guides begin with the question 'How can we get kids to do what they're told?' and then proceed to offer various techniques for controlling them. In this truly groundbreaking book, nationally respected educator Alfie Kohn begins instead by asking, 'What do kids need—and how can we meet those needs?'" Amazon.com

No Contest: The Case Against Competition Why We Lose in our Race to Win by Alfie Kohn

Book Description:

"*No Contest*, which has been stirring up controversy since its publication in 1986, stands as the definitive critique of competition. Drawing from hundreds of studies, Alfie Kohn eloquently argues that our struggle to defeat each other — at work, at school, at play, and at home — turns all of us into losers."
    After reading this book, I felt so validated about how I feel about competition and comparing children. Julienne Marks, the author

Many Pebbles to Make a Difference

Punished by Rewards: The Trouble with Gold Stars, Incentive Plans, A's, Praise, and Other Bribes by Alfie Kohn.

Book Description:

"The basic strategy we use for raising children, teaching students, and managing workers can be summarized in six words: Do this and you'll get that. We dangle goodies (from candy bars to sales commissions) in front of people in much the same way we train the family pet. Drawing on a wealth of psychological research, Alfie Kohn points the way to a more successful strategy based on working with people instead of doing things to them. 'Do rewards motivate people?' asks Kohn. 'Yes. They motivate people to get rewards.' Seasoned with humor and familiar examples, *Punished By Rewards* presents an argument unsettling to hear but impossible to dismiss." Amazon.com.

The short term goal of children "doing" for their parents and for the gold star, gifts, money, etc. they would receive, was not the intrinsic (internal) long term goal I was looking for for my students, child, and grandchild. Julienne Marks

What new and interesting concepts the last two books had for me which I shared with the parents I worked with! Julienne Marks, the author

Also Alfie Kohn's books on Education and other topics are a must to read! Julienne Marks, the author

The Schools Our Children Deserve
Feel-Bad Education
The Homework Myth
The Myth of the Spoiled Child: Challenging the Conventional Wisdom about Children and Parenting

161

I have read most of Alfie Kohn's books. He finds many research articles and then explains his premise. I respect his honesty and standing up for what he believes even when it is not what most people in our society believe in. Julienne Marks, the author

Kids, Parents and Power Struggles: Winning for a Lifetime by Mary Sheedy Kurcinka

Book Description:

"The author offers creative techniques for using power struggles as pathways to better understanding within any family. Drawing on her clinical experience with numerous real-life families, Kurcinka builds up an image of the parent as an 'emotion coach,' whose role is to build a strong, connected 'team' by understanding the players' strengths and weaknesses and showing by instruction and example how best to play the game." Amazon.com

I liked that the author feels we are the "emotion coach" of our child. We only see the behavior. We need to find out below the behavior what the underlying emotion is. Julienne Marks

Raising Your Spirited Child by Mary Sheedy Kurcinka

Book Description:

"The spirited child—often called 'difficult' or 'strong will-ed'—possesses traits we value in adults yet find challenging in children. Research shows that spirited children are wired to be 'more'; by temperament, they are more intense, sensitive, perceptive, persistent, and more uncomfortable with change than the average child. In this newly revised third edition of the award-winning classic, Kurcinka provides vivid examples of

real-life challenges and a refreshingly positive viewpoint."
Amazon.com

I felt this book was for all parents to read about their children, and themselves, not only the "Spirited Ones." I actually wrote this to the author plus how helpful the book was to me regarding myself and my child but I did not receive a reply. Julienne Marks, the author

Connection Parenting: Parenting Through Connection Instead of Coercion, Through Love Instead of Fear by Leo

Book Description:

"*Connection Parenting* is based on the parenting series Pam Leo has taught for nearly 20 years. Pam's premise is that every child's greatest emotional need is to have a strong emotional bond with at least one adult. When we have a bond with a child we have influence with a child. Pam teaches us that when we strengthen our parent-child bond we meet the child's need for connection and our need for influence." Amazon.com

Spinning Tales, Weaving Hope: Stories of Peace, Justice & the Environment, edited by Brody, Goldspinner, Green, Leventhal and Porcino of Stories for World Change Network.

Book Description:

"29 wondrous children's stories from around the world. From the mythic and the fantastic, to the silly and the serious, these timeless tales encourage conflict resolution, compassion, and sensitivity to the Earth and all living things." Amazon.com

I have shared several of these excellent stories in my *programs*. Julienne Marks, the author

A Mind at a Time by Dr. Mel Levine

Book Description:

"Defines eight specific mind systems (attention, memory, language, spatial ordering, sequential ordering, motor, higher thinking, and social thinking). Levine also incorporates scientific research to show readers how the eight neurodevelopmental systems evolve, interact, and contribute to a child's success in school." Amazon.com

After reading this book, I realized that others, like the author, may have difficulties with doing some things, (for example, using scissors) as I have. Julienne Marks, the author

The Continuum Concept In Search Of Happiness Lost
by Jane Liedloff

Book Description:

"Jean Liedloff, an American writer, spent two and a half years in the South American jungle living with Stone Age Indians. The experience demolished her Western preconceptions of how we should live and led her to a radically different view of what human nature really is. She offers a new understanding of how we have lost much of our natural well-being and shows us practical ways to regain it for our children and for ourselves." Amazon.com

Last Child in the Woods: Saving our Children from Nature Deficit Disorder by Richard Louv

Book Description:

'I like to play indoors better 'cause that's where all the electrical outlets are,' reports a fourth-grader. Never before in history have children been so plugged in-and so out of touch with the natural world. In this groundbreaking new work, child advocacy expert Richard Louv directly links the lack of nature in the lives of today's wired generation-he calls it nature deficit-to some of the most disturbing childhood trends, such as rises in obesity, Attention Deficit Disorder (ADD), and depression." Amazon.com

A friend of mine read this book in a adult gardening book discussion group. (Thanks, Vicki) Julienne Mark, the author

Breakthrough Parenting: A Revolutionary New Way to Raise Children by Jayne Major

Book Description:

"Children are beautiful jewels that have been entrusted to our care. We have a choice to polish the jewels to their natural brilliance or to dim them. By appreciating and working with the multifaceted talents of our children, we enable them to reach their greatest potential." Amazon.com

Positive Discipline by Jane Nelsen

Book Description:

"The key to positive discipline is not punishment, she tells us, but mutual respect. Nelsen coaches parents and teachers to be both firm and kind, so that any child–from a three-year-old toddler to a rebellious teenager–can learn creative cooperation and self-discipline with no loss of dignity." Amazon.com

This book is based on the teachings of Alfred Adler and Rudolf Dreikurs

I found *Positive Discipline* and *Breakthrough Parenting* very similar to Dr. Ginott and Faber and Mazlish's books and philosophy. Julienne Marks, the author

The Mister Rogers Parenting Resource Book: Helping to Understand and Encourage Your Child by Fred Rogers

Book Description:

"Two essential guides for parents, *The Mister Rogers Parenting Book* and *Mister Rogers' Playtime,* are combined into one essential, value-priced volume. This is the last book Fred Rogers worked on before his death in 2003. In this book he wanted to support parents in their most important work of parenting and to help them better understand their young children.

Written by the late Fred Rogers, one of the most trusted names in children's television, these award-winning titles provide an authoritative and encouraging reference for concerned parents. Informed by a lifetime of study in child development and years of communicating with children, this incredible resource addresses many parenting situations, from everyday concerns like a dentist's visit to such challenges as divorce and death. It also draws on Mister Rogers' unique experiences with child's play, presenting more than 80 activities that any adult can happily engage in with preschoolers." Amazon.com 'if we can bring our children understanding, comfort, and hopefulness when they need this kind of support, then they are more likely to grow into adults who can find these resources within themselves later on.' from the introduction.

Some of Mister Rogers' Children's Books/*Series*

First Experiences:
Going to the Potty
Going to the Hospital
Going on an Airplane
Going to Day Care
Going to the Dentist
Going to the Doctor
Making Friends
When a Pet Dies
Moving
The New Baby
Let's Talk About It:
Divorce
When You Have a Child in Day Care
Adoption
Extraordinary Friends
Stepfamilies
When Your Child Goes to the Dentist
Talking With Families About Creativity
Talking With Families About Discipline
When Your Child Goes to School

Other Materials by and about Fred Rogers

You are Special: Words of Wisdom for All Ages from a Beloved Neighbor by Fred Rogers

Julienne Marks

The World According to Mister Rogers: Important Things to Remember by Fred Rogers.
Peaceful Neighbor, Discovering the Countercultural Mister Rogers by Michael Long
"I can honestly say that anyone who does anything to help a child in this life is a hero to me." *Fred Rogers' Heroes: Who's Helping America's Children?*

An Article

8 Things about Mister Rogers' Neighborhood that You Want. You Do. You Want Them.

       Fred Rogers is one of my heroes. Julienne Marks, the author
       I listen to Mister Rogers' CDs or read his books when I feel alone in my thinking or need support. Julienne Marks, the author

Free to Be You and Me, Book and CD by Marlo Thomas
An article: *Free to Be... You and Me* Forty Years Later

Book Description:

"Celebrating individuality and challenging stereotypes empowers both children and adults with the freedom to be who they want to be and to have compassion and empathy for others who may be different through inspirational stories, songs, and poems." Amazon.com

       I have used this book and CD in my classroom and during my *library programs.* They talk to my heart. Julienne Marks, the author

CDs and SINGERS

I have used many of the following CDs in my *programs*. The children and parents seem to enjoy them and ask to sing them again and again. I would make copies of the lyrics and the children and parents were very grateful to use them. I would collect them at the end of the *program*.

Most of the CDs already listed throughout the **Chapters** of this Book are not repeated here.

"Peter Alsop is an educational psychologist who writes great songs for kids, a national lecturer, humorist and motivational speaker, winner of eight Best Children's Album awards and a Dad with an open mind and a sense of humor."

I used *Take Me With You* (came with lyrics) in many of my *programs* especially the songs *I'm a Little Cookie* and *Kids' Peace Song*.

Teaching Peace CD by Red Grammer

I used *I Think You're Wonderful* from *Teaching Peace* often in my *programs* as it has so much meaning. For example, I used it in my **Story Time** from Babies-School age and at the beginning of a session of the *Parenting Communication Workshops, How To Talk So Kids Will Listen™* and *Siblings Without Rivalry™* both by Adele Faber and Elaine Mazlish. The children and parents love it. I received so many compliments about this song. I ask the older children and adults to point to whom they have come with when they sing the chorus of *I Think You're Wonderful*. Other favorites from *Teaching Peace* include *Places in the World, Use a Word, See Me Beautiful*, (I used this song for the first *Parenting Communication Workshops, How To Talk So Kids Will Listen™* and *Sibling With Rivalry™* both by *Adele Faber and Elaine Mazlish)* and "*Lis-*

ten." These songs say so much, are moving, and fun to sing along with.

From the Artist:

"When Kathy and I were writing these songs we realized that "Peace" has to be something alive and vibrant or no one will ever show up for it. Our goal was to bring joy and energy to the skills we all have to learn to be good world citizens. Judging from the response of children, parents, and teachers all over the world... we were on to something!"

Teaching Peace Songbook & Teacher's Guide by Kathy Grammer.

"Combines piano, guitar and vocal arrangements of the *Teaching Peace* songs with the critically acclaimed *Teaching Peace Teacher's Guide* and a bibliography of over 100 related books. Ideal for classroom teachers, music teachers, the child who plays piano or guitar, or just loves to sing. Wonderful songs to sing for the whole family."

I heard Red Grammer at a children's concert and he was wonderful.

"Jack Hartmann's CDs come with the written lyrics. Jack Hartmann has written and recorded over 500 songs for children on 25 albums. His highly regarded educational songs are used by teachers and sung by children in schools all across the United States and around the world."

I have used his songs in many of my *programs* from the following CDs. *Getting Better at Getting Along, Learning to Love, Follow a Dream*, and *I've Got Music in Me. From the latter* CD I have used *One Small Voice* (a very moving song), *Be the Best You Can Be*, and *Riding on the Bus* (an hysterical take on the traditional *Wheels on the Bus*)

Many Pebbles to Make a Difference

Little Thinker

Using a CD and blank coloring/activity book, *Little Thinker* encourages your child to use their imagination. There is a narrator, Nancy who talks about different topics in a fun way and gives the children time to draw what she had been describing while she plays some music. Topics include: Dinosaurs, The Old West, manners and morals, safety, animals, outer space, fun poems about the sea, circus, weather, Supersites in America, travel including history of transportation, sports, life on the farm, desert, planet earth, music including different instruments, people on the job, and Christmas. When my husband and I were working on the "Long Island Explorium," (please see My Book, *Education in Different Environments,* under Museums) we were living in New York but planning on moving shortly to Florida. We had heard that the *Little Thinker Series* was released through a company called Jerome Enterprises based in Florida. On one of our trips to Florida, my husband made an appointment and met with the *Little Thinker* people to talk to them about the possibility of putting the tapes into the "Explorium" for the children to hear and draw. My husband enjoyed talking with the staff. Unfortunately, it didn't work out.

My daughter and grandson really enjoyed listening and drawing to the *Little Thinker*. Using their imaginations, the pictures they drew were so detailed.

Feedback

"This type of toy encourages children to go outside the lines. I have many fond memories of long car-rides on family vacations, sitting in the back seat listening to *Little Thinker* adventures and scribbling away in my sketch book. It taught me to imagine and create a world all my own rather than what someone else had imagined in a book or TV." Noah.

171

Julienne Marks

Affirmation Cards

I had seen many commercially made Affirmation Cards. I wanted to share some cards that had some positive words on them for children and adults, that I had put together, some using I and others using You. I used different fonts and sizes, plus they were on different colors small cards. I also had a "Ways to Use the Cards/Suggestion Card" in each packet. I put them into small plastic see-through envelopes. I gave them out to friends, etc. I also sold a few.

What The Cards Said

I Bring my Specialness to Everything I Do

It is Great to be Me

You Are Great

Be Yourself

I Bring Happiness to the World

I Have Many Talents

Great Job

You Are Making a Difference in the World

I Am a Wonderful Person

You are a Unique and Special Person

I Can Handle Anything

You Have Much to Give to the World

Ways To Use the Cards: (Suggestion Card)

Read Out loud

Write It

172

Many Pebbles to Make a Difference

Give to Employees, Coworkers

Give to Family, Friends

Put in Your Monthly Bills

Put in Lunch Box, Suitcase

Display at Your Workplace

Put on the Refrigerator, Mirror

Believe It

When the Message Doesn't Seem Appropriate, Change It.

Feedback

Comments about the Affirmation Cards

"Both my husband and my children enjoy seeing which card I would put into their lunch." (a Mom)

I had a friend who used them in her Story Telling program for adults. Here are her comments:

"I had them relate a mini–story about the message on their card. The cards helped in that they enabled the gals to express themselves verbally."

Another time with another group: "This morning I used your self-esteem cards with my rehab women. I gave them each a card and had them 'tell' what their card meant to them; I am doing warm-up exercises at each session with this new group using the cards."

"They would be a wonderful way for me to end the sessions. They are useful, provocative and perfect." (Thanks, Meta)

Other Comments

Another person who used the cards had them hanging in the closet at the school she worked at. When she was having a difficult time she would run to the closet and read them for inspiration. (Thanks Peggy)

"I love, love, love the self-esteem cards."

"I enjoyed sharing your Affirmation Cards with others."

Check out the following websites for more information on this **Chapter**:

Checkout these websites for more information:

http://www.parents.com/parenting/relationships/friendship/
https://www.care.com/a/re-vitalize-date-night-1011091118,
htthttp://www.buscaglia.com/inspiration. aspx
p:// http://www.nytimes.com/1983/05/08/magazine/the-loss-of-childhood.html?pagewanted=2)
www.popsugar.com/moms/Vacation-With out-Kids-28964092
www.Amazon.com
July, 2015
http://finance.yahoo.com/news/american-education-system-no-idea-140200
954.html?soc_src=mediacontentstory&soc_trk=maput
http://www.livesinthebalance. Org /parents-families
http://www.johnholtgws.com/growing-without-schooling-issue-archive/
http://www.alfiekohn.org/contest/
http://www.fredrogers.org/parents/#sthash.WhrRhkvq.zbrTsx0j.dpuf
http://neighborhoodarchive.com/ video/other/heroes/index.html
http://icetrend.blogspot.com/2015/03/8
http://www .fred rogers. org/parents/
www.huffingtonpost.com/.../free-to-be-40-years-later_b_2206066.html

http://www.amazon.com/Free-You-Marlo-Thomas-Friends/dp/B000F2CC0E.http://peteralsop.com/about-peter
http://www.peteralsop.com/
http://www.amazon.com/Teaching-Peace-Red-Grammer/dp/B000009NGF
https://www.redgrammer.com/index.php/store/lyrics?id=110

http://www.songsforteaching.com/store/jack-hartmann-c-984.html
http://www .littlethinker adventures.com/
http://raise emright.com/toys/little-thinkers/
http://www.buscaglia.com/inspiration.aspx

Chapter 8

CONCLUSION

"Don't be satisfied with stories, how things have gone with others. Unfold your own myth." Rumi, *The Essential Rumi,* (Thanks, Elaine)

The Man, the Boy, and the Donkey, An Aesop's Fable

A Man and his son were once going with their Donkey to market. As they were walking along by its side, a country-man passed them and said: "You fools, what is a donkey for but to ride upon?"

So the Man put the Boy on the Donkey and they went on their way. But soon they passed a group of men, one of whom said: "See that lazy youngster; he lets his father walk while he rides."

So the Man ordered his Boy to get off, and got on him-self. But they hadn't gone far when they passed two women, one of whom said to the other: "Shame on that lazy man to let his poor little son trudge along."

Well, the Man didn't know what to do, but at last he took his Boy up before him on the Donkey. By this time they had come to the town, and the passers-by began to jeer and point at them. The Man stopped and asked what they were scoffing at. The men said: "Aren't you ashamed of yourself for overloading that poor donkey of yours and your hulking son?"

The Man and Boy got off and tried to think what to do. They thought and they thought, till at last they cut down a pole, tied the donkey's feet to it, and raised the pole and the donkey to their shoulders. They went along amid the laughter of all who met them till they came to Market Bridge, when the Donkey, getting one of his feet loose, kicked out and caused the Boy to drop his end of the pole. In the struggle the Donkey fell over the bridge, and his forefeet being tied together he was drowned. "That will teach you," said an old man who had followed them.

Another title for this story: "The Miller, his Son and the Donkey:" There are many different versions. I have heard one where the donkey does not die. The Moral of this Aesop's Fable "Please all and you will please none."

"You never can please all the people all the time. You can please some of the people some of the time, all of the people some of the time, some of the people all of the time but you can never please all of the people all of the time." Abraham Lincoln   There is some discussion that Abraham Lincoln may not have said this.

"The meaning of life is to find your gifts. The purpose of life is to give it away." Pablo Picasso

"I feel the real reason we are all here, our purpose of being, is to help others find their little piece of happiness and heaven right here on earth ." by Ken Poirot

This is what I have wanted to do in this book, by sharing my experiences, ideas, ideals, philosophy, *programs,* and love for children and adults.

"Love is the only way to rescue humanity from all ills." Leo Tolstoy in *Letters to a Hindi.*

Julienne Marks

The great Russian writer Leo Tolstoy had a close friendship with Mahatma Gandhi. They wrote letters to each other sharing their dedication to nonviolence.

Connections is a key component in this Book, *Many Pebbles to Make a Difference, Inspiring Ways You Can Improve Children's Lives by Making Connections, For Families, Parents, Grandparents.*

I have shared in this Book *programs* such as "Family Connection Time," and "Grandparent Connection Time." This Book also talks about *Connections* in **Chapter 1**. **Chapter 2** talks about the *Parenting Communication Workshops, How To Talk So Kids Will Listen*™ and *Siblings Without Rivalry*™ both by Adele Faber and Eaine Mazlish and the Parent Support Group which is about *connections*/bonding with your children and other parents.

A quotation I found at the restaurant, Cracker Barrel: "Be yourself but be your best self. Dare to be different and follow your own star." This is part of *Live Each Day to the Fullest* by S. H. Payer

The famous quote: "This above all: To thine own self be true" by Shakespeare helps express one of my goals for this Book.

We all have our authentic way of sharing our story. This Resource Book, Handbook, Reference Book, Instructional Book, Guide Book that you have in your hands, has shared my work life/story/experiences in "my way." The song, *My Way,* popularized by Frank Sinatra with its lyrics written by Anka, says it for me.

It is my legacy. (Thank, Pam) To me a legacy is wanting to share one's life work and contributing your gifts to others. That is what this Book is about.

"It's not what you gather, but what you scatter that tells what kind of life you have lived." Golda Meir

Put yourself, your beliefs, your goals, etc. into your *programs*. Find within yourself what works for you and what you "need" to share with others. When you find it, you will know. Then share it with others, especially the children. They need what you can share. I am sharing with you the reader because I would like you to use parts/ aspects, etc. of this Book if they resonate with you for your own *programs*.

Education of a *Wandering Man* by Louis L'Amour, page 202. Alfred Lord Tennyson said from *Ulysses*, "I am a part of all that I have met."

In this Book, I have shared my work life, my personal philosophy and numerous *programs* done in various venues. I have worked with children of all ages, parents, and teachers. By my experiences, meeting different people, and readings, I have seen what works, what doesn't, and what has resonated for me. I feel it is extremely important that we need to be kind, compassionate, empathic, appreciative, humane, and show we care for ourselves and each other, as well as, to be *connected* with others. And this is what I have shared with you in this Book. This has occurred in many of my *programs* that I present, as well as in my Presentations in this Book.

I have noticed a thread running throughout my life: encouraging all of us to help others, giving back what we have learned, and to feel good about ourselves.

"In helping others we shall help ourselves for whatever good we give out completes the circle and comes back to us." Flora Edwards.

"What counts in life is not the mere fact that we have lived. It is what difference we have made to the lives of others that will determine the significance of the life we lead."
Nelson Mandela

I hope this Book, *Many Pebbles to Make a Difference, Inspiring Ways You Can Improve Children's Lives by Making Connections, For Families, Parents, Grandparents* with its **Agendas** and **PR (Public Relations)** of *programs*, comments from participants, **(Feedback)** book titles, ***Mrs. Marks' Sparks,*** my philosophy, ideas etc. will be a Resource Book, HandBook Reference Book, Instructional Book, Guide Book, for you as you strive to share YOUR *programs* and philosophy.

"As human beings, our job in life is to help people realize how rare and valuable each one of us really is, that each of us has something that no one else has-or ever will have-something inside that is unique to all time. It's our job to encourage each other to discover that uniqueness and to provide ways of developing its expressions." Fred Rogers

"Julienne, I love how caring and involved you stay in anything you do. Thank you for working so hard to make this world a better place for all." (Thanks, Lee)

I hope this Book will be of help to you on your journey of making a difference in the world through "YOUR" *programs*. And through these *programs* you will find others (sources, *programs)* that will suit you. My best wishes to you on your quest to being authentically/genuinely YOU, being your best, and then sharing this with children and adults. I would be very interested in knowing how this Book has helped you on your journey. If you would like to share what you have done with the *programs* and how you have made them yours, etc., I can be reached at heron52@bellsouth.net.

I believe being a parent is the most important job we have. It is filled with joy and yet it is difficult and challenging. Support (not isolation) is needed for this very important job. *Family Matters: Parenting is the Most Important Job Ever* by Diana Boggia. Posted Feb. 2, 2012.

As I began the Book with Quotations, I will end the final **Chapter** of this Book, with my father's favorite quotation, a Traditional Gaelic blessing.

May The Road Rise Up To Meet You
"May the road rise up to meet you.
May the wind be always at your back.
May the sun shine warm upon your face;
the rains fall soft upon your fields
and until we meet again,
may G-d hold you in the palm of His hand."

Check out the following websites for more information on topics discussed in this **Chaper.**

http://www.goodreads.com/author/quotes/875661.Rumi.
http://www.taleswithmorals. com /aesop-fable-the-man-the-boy-and-the-donkey.htm
http://www.brainyquote.com/quotes/quotes/a/abrahamlin11034 0.html
http://isp.netscape.com/whatsnew/ pack age.jsp?name=fte/lincoln/lincoln
http://www.goodreads.com/quotes/607827-the-meaning-of-life-is-to-find-your-gift-the
http://www.goodreads.com/quotes/tag/purpose-of-life?page=2
https://www.brainpickings.org/2014/08/21/leo-tolstoy-gandhi-letter-to-a-hindu/
www.islandtimemassage.com.au/blog/power-vs-love.
http://www.anxietyslayer.com/help-with-anxiety-podcasts /2010/6/30/poem-live-each-day-to-the-fullest.html
www.metrolyrics.com/my-way-lyrics-paul-anka .html
For more information about a legacy, please check out these websites
http://www.huffingtonpost.com/joan-moran/5-ways-to-leave-a-great-l_b_7148112.html
and http://www.legacyproject.org/guides/whatislegacy.html.
http://humfer.net/goldameir/index.html
http://humfer.net/goldameir/index.html
 http://thinkexist.com/quotation/in_helping_others-we_shall_help_ourselves-for/7843.html
http://www.goodreads.com/quotes/829582-what-counts-in-life-is-not-the-mere-fact-that
http://www.goodreads.com/quotes/913279-as-human-beings-our-job-in-life-is-to-help
http://www.cantonrep.com/article/20120 202/News/302029836

http://www.worldprayers.org/archive/prayers/invocations/may_
the_road_rise_up.html
http://www.enotes.com/shakespeare-quotes/thine-own-self-true
https://meridianlifedesign.com/about-legacy/what-is-legacy/
http://humfer.net/goldameir/index.html

Julienne Marks

MY ACKNOWLEDGEMENTS/THANK YOUS

This page is for me to thank the many people who have helped me in my life journey in so many ways. Thank you for your encouragement to help me be the best me I can be, being true to myself, being authentically me, and you advocating for me. I am so grateful and fortunate to have met and been touched by so many. I may be sharing some of your ideas. Thank you for being you and sharing with me who you are. If I have forgotten anyone, which I am sure I inadvertently did, please know you are in my heart. I apologize and ask for your understanding. I also apologize for sometimes forgetting your first name through the many years that have gone by. Even with people who have passed on, I wrote to them in this thank you page as "you" as that is how I see them listening from heaven. I am only using first names.

For your information, these acknowledgements pertain primarily with parents and does not deal with people I have worked with at schools or libraries or with peace educators. These can be found in My three other Books, *Education in Different Environments, Reading And Books* and *Multiculturalism And Peace.*

Thank you to **Stu**, my husband, who has wanted me to write this Book for many years. You have supported and encouraged me to write this Book. I so appreciate the many things you did for me so I could work on the Book (and other things) like meals, clothes buying, cleaning, gas, etc. It was wonderful to be able to brainstorm with you about my work and this Book. You would say to me, "I never know what I would be coming home to or what to expect from you: another job or project/passion/cause. You were never in the mainstream." When someone asked him if he had read my Book, he answered, "I lived it right alongside of her." You actually have lived my work life with me helping me from setting up my

184

classrooms and coming home early from our vacations to putting pictures up and off of the walls of the libraries. I so enjoyed working and being a co-chairperson with you in the *Parenting Communication Workshops, How To Talk So Kids Will Listen*™ and *Siblings Without Rivalry*™ both by Adele Faber and Elaine Mazlish. It's been quite a Ride!

Thank you to my caring parents, **Leonard R. Levy**, who was organized, (I loved dancing with you) and **Esther Levy** with her interest in the arts, enjoying art museums, classical music, caring for others. My parents taught me, "If you can't say anything nice, don't say anything at all " (from Bambi) which has its pluses and minuses. My Mom would often say that "the best time of her life is the time she is in right now" which I try and remember.

Thank you to **Elissa**, my daughter, who is beautiful inside and out. What a Mom! Watching you with Ethan, moves me so! All that you have taught him is incredible like caring for Bailey, his honesty, his sensitivity, his love. He is so excited about you reading *The Harry Potter Series* with your English accent. Your caring for others shows in your work. You relate to your theatre high school students so incredibly well. Many students and their parents say that you are the reason for their child's self-confidence and /or going on stage or becoming a drama teacher. How you put on a musical from auditions, seeing which students are best for which role, to blocking, to dancing/singing, to costumes to lights, to scenery to makeup to opening night is amazing to see. I am sure it was not easy, me being your mother. For example, having a driving teacher for a year as I was too nervous to drive with you which was my problem, not yours and your one friend, (Thanks, Anne) being the first to go to the Mall alone with, drive with, sleep over, etc. because I trusted her. And all the schools I put you into as I was always on my lookout for the best one for you. Thanks also, for all the Technology help you gave me and not laughing at me. I enjoy our talks.

Thank you to **Ethan**, my grandson who loves reading, drama, (and all that includes acting, singing and dancing) sports, chess, animals, art, and enjoys so many things: as paleontology, Pokémon, the elements, origami, writing books, science, and making "concoctions." After books you have read or movies you have seen, you MUST make a costume out of boxes, etc. of one of the characters you saw like a knight, chipmunk, spaceship, a racecar, etc. (with Papa's help).

Thank you to **Dana**, my daughter-in-law, whose calmness helps me out so much. Your love for my Elissa, my daughter and Ethan, my grandson is so wonderful to see. From playing with him, camping out, to making up Bunny stories, going on rides at Six Flags, etc. he loves it so!

My Siblings:

Thank you to **Bill**, already an author with several books under your belt, who wanted me to write this Book for so long. You encouraged me with outlines and ideas. I was lucky to have you to run things past as you have already gone through them as an author. I appreciate our deep talks. I am really me with you.

Thank you to nurturing **Marlene** who would listen to my frustrations over the writing of this Book and life in general. We grew up together in Florida as Moms which I am so grateful for and celebrated all those holidays together at your home. I am so glad you liked to entertain. I was so honored that you attended one of the *Parenting Communication Workshops, How To Talk So Kids Will Listen*™ by Adele Faber and Elaine Mazlish. You listened to me.

Thank you to nurturing **Marsha** who lived in California and would listen to me talk about the *programs* I was sharing and everything else. You made things for me such as the work gloves for the story of *The Enormous Turnip* and worked out on the computer my **Agenda** for *"Connect to the World at Your Library,"* a talk I gave to the library staff. You listened to me."

Thank you to my encouraging cousin who was/is like my older sister, **Jo-Ann.** Our phone calls and visits helped to continue our strong relationship. Your encouragement of being who I am is/was important to me.

Thank you to my brother's daughter, **Michelle**, who early on, read this Book and made some great comments for me to work on plus, you fixed up the fonts, formatting, and spacing. You wrote to me, "Your ideas behind the manuscript are amazing and your passion is evident." Your love of animals and caring for others is wonderful to see.

Thank you to my other nieces and nephews:
Diana with such a large heart for others working with immigrant people. I honor you. With all that is going on in our world you are needed.
Lee whom I saw grow up with Elissa and we wrote a book together on planes. I enjoyed our special relationship.
Errol who is the proud father of three children and a wonderful son to my sister.
Shoshana, who I honor for being a vegetarian for many years and such a great teacher to young children.

Thank you to **Uncle Hal** and **Aunt Joanne** who gave Stu and I such great support in our early married years. You really listened to me and supported me to be the best ME I could be.

Thank you to **Janice.** I am happy to see how wonderful you and my brother are together.

Thank you to **Terry** and **Jimmy** and all the support you have given to Elissa, Dana and Ethan. Terry your cooking is FABULOUS!

Thank you to **Inez** who would watch my brother, sisters, and me when my parents went on vacation. You listened to me and gave me attention.

To the religious people in my life who taught me about Judaism. Thank you to **Rabbi Katz** (who presided at my Bat

Mitzvah, Confirmation, marriage, my daughter's naming,) (friend of your daughter, Debbie), **Cantor Altman** who had a magnificent voice (my Bat Mitzvah, Confirmation, marriage, and my Father's funeral), and **Rabbi Skiddell** who actually called me when I made an inquiry about the synagogue, who drove to our Kibbutz in Israel several times to see us, and presided at my daughter's Bat Mitzvah both in Israel and at the synagogue. I won at a silent auction a copy of Andrew Wyatt, *Christina's World* that was his, that I adore. Thank you to **Bella**, cantorial soloist and friend, whose voice lifted me up so much.

Thank you to **Dr. Haim Ginott,** author of *Between Parent and Child* who was the impetus to my own Parenting philosophy. You validated so much of what I felt but which was unfortunately not contemporary. Your humane philosophy of *communication* between parent and child (his title) started me on my parenting journey. Before I would be the chairperson for each *Parenting Communication Workshop, How To Talk So Kids Will Listen™* and *Siblings Without Rivalry™* both by Adele Faber and Elaine Mazlish, I would reread your books and keep saying to myself Right On! What Dr. Ginott wrote was so true for me.

Thank you to **Zelda Gross**, who studied with Dr. Ginott and gave a Parent Support Group that Stu, my husband and I attended, beginning when Elissa, our daughter, was two. It helped us tremendously on our parenting journey then and now. This Parent Support Group was the beginning for me presenting the *Parenting Communication Workshops* of Adele Faber and Elaine Mazlish's *How To Talk So Kids Will Listen™* and *Siblings without Rivalry™* and to also begin a Parent Support Group in our home.

Thank you to **Adele Faber** and **Elaine Mazlish** who are the authors of *How To Talk So Kids Will Listen and Listen So Kids Will Talk* and *Siblings Without Rivalry* and their workshop kits that I have been sharing with parents for many years.

I love hearing their expressive voices on the CDs and enjoy the way the workshops kits were put together, first having the parents experience what their children might be feeling, then practicing at the workshop, using the skills at home, and then sharing with the other participants how their week went with the new skills.

Thank you to **Leslie Faber**, Adele's husband, whom I talked to and had a delightful conversation with about his wife's books and workshops.

Friends are very important to me. My friends have supported, challenged, and motivated me to be the best me I can be at different times of my life by listening and encouraging me. My friends and I would talk deeply and meaningfully. On our journey through life one meets, says hello, and perhaps goodbye to friends. I met some at school, as a young parent, at work, others from a synagogue, and from groups, and businesses I attended.

Thank you to **Carla** who in Middle School was my friend. I enjoyed learning about your heritage.

Thank you to my Merrick, N.Y., friends **Laura** and **Roz**. You were my High School friends and we still keep in touch.

Laura, whom I needed to learn to stop being so possessive of. We love to laugh. It was great sharing our memories of high school and sharing our adult lives.

Roz, whom I traveled to Washington D.C. with while in college. I was so scared.

Both of you really listened to me. We all went through our teen years together.

Thank you to **Cathy** whom I knew through our Dads, both of whom were dentists. Later on in life we began corresponding. When I would see your handwriting on a letter, I would be so excited to hear about you and your life.

Thank you to my College friends:

Char, my roommate who was so wonderful to me although I was so homesick. I will never forget the bat in our bedroom.

Lynn, who became my friend in my new college and included me with her friends.

Alice, who was a good friend in college.

Thank you to **Mina (Lee's Mom)**, whom I met at a preschool as a young Mom and who told me about "A Parenting Support Group" which Stu and I attended based on Dr. Ginott's work led by Zelda Gross.

Thank you to **Pat and John,** our next door neighbors who were the greatest neighbors we could have asked for, helping us out in times of need and just having fun together.

Thank you to **Debbie** whose daughter and husband were also in Indian Princess as mine were. We became good friends.

Thank you to **Dolores,** Elissa's babysitter, and more a friend who did plays, (Remember Rumpelstiltskin?) cooked, played, read books, and tried cleaning up with her. ("Oh, no problem Mr. Meims will clean it up.") What a friendship! Elissa still stays in contact.

Thank you to my special helpers on my journey through my life: **Mrs. Stern, Bonnie, Maddie, Cynthia, Marta, John, Lana**, **Tom** and others. You all helped me to see the real me.

Thank you to **Missy** who is a great listener, shared some pearls of wisdom, and supported me for who I am.

Thank you to all the supportive parents from my teaching days.

Caroleen who was my friend and the parent of two of my students. I learned much from you.

Joyce who also was the parent of two of my students.

Jennifer's Mom, who was supportive of my teaching .

Bob's parents who sent me a photograph of Bob and his child. I was amazed looking at his photograph of this man as I remembered him as a boy.

John's parents, who invited Stu, my husband and I to dinner (I asked my principal if I should accept) and find out they went to school together.

Thank you to **Marna,** an author, who helped me in the very beginning stages of writing this Book. She said that I needed to share my *programs* and the input I received about them, my philosophy, and who I am. She helped me to organize the Book. I savored working with you and Nemo.

Two Friends read one of my first versions of this Book. (Other friends wanted to also.) Thank you to **Nancy** for reading my Book. You wrote, "I thought your book was amazing. I have learned a great deal from your writing. I love how you explain how to engage children in activities."

Thank you to **Mae** for reading My Book. You said, "I have so much respect for you, Julienne! I am amazed at all the education you have and how you have used it in the world of children and parents and teachers. Your book has so many good ideas for teachers and parents. I love that you are such a promoter of peace. I so enjoyed reading about your different *programs.* "

Thank you to **Lee,** who encouraged me to be me and said "Remember that the world needs your book to be published."

Thank you to **Lea,** what a support you have been to me. What energy you have. What good you are doing for the world. I enjoyed the "Precious Stone" story you shared with me. Please see My Book, *Multiculturalism And Peace,* for a website where you can find this story.

Thank you to **Ada,** whose encouragement, support, and really "seeing me" is so appreciated. You would write me on days you thought would affect me due to my sensitivity. For example: when the shootings of Sandy Hook occurred and my retirement party. You understood my dislike of driving and you drove far often so we could meet, talk and listen to each other. We felt so similarly about books and children. What a compliment to me that you used some of my *programs* with your twist to it which is exactly the goal of this Book for the reader to do.

Thank you to **Pam,** whom I met at my first apartment where one brought their garbage. We fast became friends. We walked together, danced, and talked and listened to each other. Then you moved back to Minnesota (the snow there is amazing), and we talk as often as we can. We were both using Richard Simmons CDs and laughing. I appreciate your support with this Book.

Thank you to **Ginny** who organized, listened and, trusted me. You put together the themed folders and notebooks.

Interestingly, I met two Moms who were named **Julie:** Thank you to **Julie** and **Eric,** whom I delighted in sharing **Story Time** with your sons and seeing them grow. What a teacher, Julie you are! I relished you asking me for book titles on different themes.

Thank you to **Julie** who attended my **Story Time** with your first daughter and then your two daughters and the *Parenting Communication Workshop, How To Talk So Kids Will Listen™* by Adele Faber and Elaine Mazlish. We talked and really listened to each other. What a gift that was for me.

Thank you to **Carrie,** whose child was in my "Baby Story Times" and would sit on my lap. I appreciate your support for me.

Thank you to **Amber** who wrote a letter to the Director of the Library system about me. What a pleasure your children are. I adored them.

Thank you to **Nancy** and our deep talks even now. Your love and support are felt deeply. Thanks for visiting us.

Kathalyn and our deep talks even now. I felt I could always talk to you. Thanks for visiting us.

Shelly whom I met at a *Waldorf School,* then again at the School I was their Media Specialist, and our studying together on Saturdays. It was so wonderful continuing to bump into each other.

Andy, my supervisor and friend who taught me about calmness, encouraging me to be my best, and how to gently supervise by listening and encouraging. Driving a1 ½ hour one way was surely worth it to work with him.

Marianne, author of so many incredible children's books. I honor you so. We had deep talks about children's books. Thank you for all your support and help when we worked together.

Rose What a friend, a great listener. I enjoyed going to our place for lunch and our talks. Many of your videos you sent me were so uplifting and soul searching.

Maria whom I knew both in Florida and Georgia. It was very surrealistic being with you in both places as librarians. I have so enjoyed our friendship.

Gretta. How great to reconnect after so many years. What a wonderful friend!

Jo, my supervisor who let me be me. Your door was always open to me. I am so grateful for you and having another great supervisor as I again drove for an hour one way. I enjoyed attending your church with you.

Vicki After Retirement, we became friends sharing about our grandchildren and children.

Watching you **Julia**, my friend, my teacher, grow, thank you for your patience with me. What a team we made. Working together on the Fairs was great. I honor you so. I so enjoy watching you and your son. You look so great with heels. What accomplishments you have achieved!

Deborah You were so kind to me. I will never forget that. I cannot get over all the classroom materials you have at your home.

Leigh Our peanut butter and bananas lunches, my jewelry breaking and we would crackup so. I loved laughing with you. You are so artistic and talented. I am so happy I have two of your pieces of artwork of Ethan. Thanks for being my friend.

Kathleen Your deepness inspires me. I loved going to the Buddhist Temple with you and listening to birds. What a pleasure to get to know your Mom and your children and grandchildren.

Rhonda, I so enjoyed meeting at our place and hearing about you, belly dancing, and reenactments.

Susan. I remember our deep talks and the walk we took on the Silver Comet Trail and how safe I felt with you. It was so beautiful there.

Carmella. I enjoyed having you a part of the Women's Group and meeting at your wonderful home. I so like your saying, "everything is lovely."

Thank you, **Mae**. Our friendship began at **Story Time** when you sent me some quotations. Then we talked and listened to each other. I found out you had homeschooled your four children. I so honor you. Our friendship continued to grow as we shared each other's weeks. You gave me such interesting books to read. You have published a children's book. Again I honor you. Your saying, "It'll be fine!" is helpful to me.

Some parents I have stayed in touch with after sharing the *Parenting Communication Workshops, How To Talk So Kids Will Listen*™ and *Siblings Without Rivalry*™ both by Adele Faber and Elaine Mazlish.

Thank you to **Laura** who attended five times. I relished our deep talks.

Thank you, **Margaret** whom I am so glad I met you and your lovely family. You took the "Conflict Resolution for Families," attended **Story Time**, had us over for a delicious meal and company, and attended the Women's and Parent Support Group.

Thank you, **Sarah** for inviting me to your Mom's Group. I appreciate you doing the Evites for the Parenting Support Group.

Thank you, **Sarah** for allowing me to get to know your lovely family and feeling your constant support.

Two Moms That I Passed the Torch To for the *Parenting Communication Workshops, How To Talk So Kids Will Listen™* and *Siblings Without Rivalry™* both by Adele Faber and Elaine Mazlish.

Thank you to **Devyan**i. I enjoyed getting to know your culture and your spiritualness. I relished our deep discussions. I reveled in working with you on the *Parenting Communication Workshop, How To Talk So Kids Will Listen™ and Siblings Without Rivalry™* by Adele Faber and Elaine Mazlish. I appreciate you wanting me at your daughters' school, then had me at your Temple to share the *Parenting Communication Workshop, How To Talk So Kids Will Listen™* and *Siblings Without Rivalry™* both by Adele Faber and Elaine Mazlish. I am so glad you found the themed folders and notebooks helpful. Thank you for the beautiful Nutcracker.

Thank you, **Anne**. I have savored seeing your daughters grow. I remember when you offered to have your husband make copies for the **Agendas** for the **Story Time**. I reveled in working with you on the *Parenting Communication Workshops, How To Talk So Kids Will Listen™* and *Sibling Without Rivalry™* both by Adele Faber and Elaine Mazlish. I appreciate you doing the Evites for the Parenting Support Group. Thank your daughters for the Jack-in- the Box which I use.

Homeschooling Moms

I enjoyed getting to know you and your children and the different ways you homeschooled/unschooled

I enjoyed knowing your children. Seeing your children grow was a treat for me. I enjoyed our talks about books, homeschooling, and life. Thank you **Moira, Kathy, Jonica, Lynn,** and **Barbara.**

Thank you to my special friends, **Phyllis** and her son, **Steven** and all you both have accomplished. I am glad we are still keeping in touch.

Thank you, **Samantha.** Meeting someone who had been homeschooled was such a treat for me. I found our talks so interesting. I enjoyed knowing your children. When you daughter came up to sing with me at the end of **Story Time,** what a great feeling. I loved coming to your home for lunch. How special it was.

Thank you, **Jamie.** I enjoyed our talks. I so relished knowing your children. I adored hearing you play the violin. I still use the music box you gave me. What fun having lunch with you and your children.

It was so interesting that two of the homeschooled Moms I knew were named Julie.

Thank you, **Julie,** with such adorable children who gave great kisses. We talked quite a bit about homeschooling and teaching. After I retired I met you at the Central Library. How wonderful to see you and the children and watching them grow. I really like the *Raggedy Ann* book you gave me.

Julie with two sons who loved reading to Nemo. I enjoyed knowing your children. Seeing your children grow was a treat for me. I enjoyed our talks about books, homeschooling, and life. Knowing your family was a gift for me.

Thank you, **Cathie.** You were one of the first parents I met. Your children attended many of my *programs,* I adored them all especially Megan who kept me on my toes. She so loved to talk books.

Thank you, **Barbara,** I savored hearing your daughter read to Nemo. I enjoyed seeing your children grow. Thank you for inviting me to your daughter's birthday party. I relished our breakfasts and our deep talks.

Thank you, **Brand**i, for your support and friendship. Knowing your daughter is a delight. Having breakfast/lunch with her was so much fun. I also enjoyed our deep talks. And that delicious chocolate cake you brought to my party. I so relished her reading to Nemo and her laughter. I will never forget how you traveled to East Cobb for a *program* I was doing there.

Thank you to **Glenda**, my ballet teacher who encouraged me to go on Toe as an adult and I actually performed a Toe solo at the recital.

Thank you to **Linda**, my ballet and interpretative dance teacher, friend, and spiritual teacher and dance teacher of Elissa.

Thank you, **Jackie**, my dance teacher and friend who is so patient with me. I loved the ballet dancing and talking.

Thank you, **Sally,** and our new friendship, your tremendous support and encouragement of who I am.

Thank you to **Shanelle,** who helped me in more ways than you know.

Thank you to **Shelly,** who found us three homes in three years. You attended my parties.

Thank you, **Shellie,** my first friend in Georgia. You helped me a tremendous amount on the job. Your understanding was wonderful .

Thank you to **Jan.** Your talent in music and sharing it with the children was so inspirational. I learned so much from you.

Thank you to **Valerie**. I knew you in two ways, one as a parent who brought her children to *programs* and as a talented music teacher. I learned much from you.

Thank you to **Hadara** from Israel. Your friendship while we were in Israel and afterwards is something I treasure. Your warm welcome and making sure we were comfortable in our two homes was so hospitable. I relished your letters and our talks. Your popcorn was the best I ever had.

Thank you to my hairdressers **Pat, Sue, Ezat** who not only did my hair but listened and talked with me.

Thank you to **Judy,** my new friend from Head Start. You saw my sensitivity and vulnerability and you gave me an Angel scarf to protect me. I was touched.

Thank you to **Elaine** who supported me in the *Parenting Communication Workshop, How To Talk So Kids Will Listen*™ by Adele Faber and Elaine Mazlish. You gave me a lovely perfumed oil and we had deep talks.

Thank you to **Paula**, I loved working with you. Thanks for your CD player help. I so appreciate the help you gave me with my book technologically. You never laughed at me.

Thank you to **Yuri** for wanting to help me technologically. Your kindness and support are appreciated .

Thank you to my publishers, **Nadine** and **Farris** of Yawn's Publishing. You supported and helped me take a 600-page book and make it into four books. Thank you for your kindness and not laughing at all the tech and writing help I needed.

Thank you to my three cats: **Kat**, (Main Coon) **Butterscotch**, (Calico who lived for 20 years) and **Peaches** (a Tabby who spoke all the time and brings us balls and a shoe lace to throw) Although quite different, all brought me much joy.

Thank you to **Bailey**, my daughter's dog we have had so much fun.

Books in the **Many Pebbles to Make a Difference:** Inspiring Ways You Can Improve Children's Lives by Making Connections *series:*

For Families, Parents, Grandparents

Education in Different Environments: *For Teachers, Librarians, Museums Educators, Parents, and All Who Work With Children*

Reading And Books: *For Parents, Teachers, Librarians, and All Who Work With Children*

Multiculturalism and Peace: *For Teachers, Librarians, Peace Educators, Parents, and All Who Work With Children*

CPSIA information can be obtained
at www.ICGtesting.com
Printed in the USA
LVOW04s0151090416
482859LV00002B/2/P